Praise for *Bullsh*

De Goey provides investors with an entertaining overview of how our brains get in the way of maximizing our financial potential. Perhaps more importantly, he links these biases to what is happening in the world around us and provides prescriptions on how to optimize our behaviour.

— Preet Banerjee, consultant to the wealth management industry and founder of MoneyGaps

Long a maverick in the Canadian financial adviser community, John De Goey's third book is an erudite exposition of how unwarranted optimism can be detrimental to the financial health of portfolios.

— Jonathan Chevreau, author, columnist, and founder of Financial Independence Hub

From broad behavioural errors to the specifics of Canadian markets, *Bullshift* offers new ways for people to evaluate their thinking and achieve better outcomes. It's packed with useful insight on how to make more informed, rational decisions.

— Dr. Cheryl Hurst, founder of equity, diversity, and inclusion corporate learning platform PeopleGaps

If you want to be money smart, read *Bullshift*. John's decades of experience, wisdom, and guidance will leave you richer.

— Kelley Keehn, bestselling author of *Talk Money to Me*

A truly wonderful read and an important book that will help so many people solve the puzzle that is understanding themselves, their money, and their behaviours.

— Dennis Moseley-Williams, founder of DMW Strategic Consulting

There's a large body of evidence that behavioural biases are a significant reason why so many investors fail to achieve their investment goals. Overconfidence is particularly deeply ingrained. We think — and are encouraged by the media and financial commentators to think — that we can do things that are beyond our sphere of competence. We're all prone to overconfidence and optimism and we need to help each other in guarding against it.

— ROBIN POWELL, journalist, author, and editor
of The Evidence-Based Investor

There's a new kind of adviser coming to the forefront of wealth management. These days, advisers who are more focused on behaviour and decisions are winning business. Understanding what drives client attitudes is a winning proposition for keeping them focused on what's important.

— CHARLIE SPIRING, ICD.D, founder and chair
of Wellington-Altus Financial Inc.

Bullshift

Bullshift

HOW OPTIMISM BIAS
THREATENS YOUR FINANCES

JOHN J. DE GOEY

DUNDURN
PRESS

Publisher: Kwame Scott Fraser | Acquiring editor: Kathryn Lane | Editor: Dominic Farrell
Cover designer: Karen Alexiou
Cover image: istock.com/Artnivora Studio
Interior cartoons: Mark Krause

Library and Archives Canada Cataloguing in Publication

Title: Bullshift : how optimism bias threatens your finances / John J. De Goey.
Names: De Goey, John J., author.
Description: Includes bibliographical references and index.
Identifiers: Canadiana (print) 20220417105 | Canadiana (ebook) 20220417121 | ISBN 9781459750906 (softcover) | ISBN 9781459750913 (PDF) | ISBN 9781459750920 (EPUB)
Subjects: LCSH: Investments. | LCSH: Finance, Personal.
Classification: LCC HG4521 .D4 2023 | DDC 332.6—dc23

We acknowledge the support of the Canada Council for the Arts and the Ontario Arts Council for our publishing program. We also acknowledge the financial support of the Government of Ontario, through the Ontario Book Publishing Tax Credit and Ontario Creates, and the Government of Canada.

Care has been taken to trace the ownership of copyright material used in this book. The author and the publisher welcome any information enabling them to rectify any references or credits in subsequent editions.

The publisher is not responsible for websites or their content unless they are owned by the publisher.

Printed and bound in Canada.

Dundurn Press
1382 Queen Street East
Toronto, Ontario, Canada M4L 1C9
dundurn.com, @dundurnpress 𝕏 f ⊙

For Olena

Contents

Introduction

BIAS IS A PART OF LIFE. We all have biases — whether we want them or not and whether we are aware of them or not. It would be unfair to criticize someone for having biases — that would be tantamount to criticizing that person for being human.

A bias may be good or bad; to judge that, it is necessary to consider the consequences if someone acts on that bias. The thing is, though, acting on some biases can, depending on the circumstances, produce different kinds of consequences. So, making judgments about the positive or negative nature of different kinds of bias is not always easy to do. In any case, it is unfair to impugn someone's character simply because they have biases.

It's entirely reasonable to expect professionals, no matter what field they work in, to act with honour. They should be expected to go about their business in a way that is proper, rational, and ethical — and almost all professionals (financial advisers, doctors, dentists, lawyers, accountants, teachers, engineers, et cetera) intend to do good work using the best evidence available to them. Like the rest of us, however, professionals are subject to different kinds and different amounts of bias — conscious and unconscious. Obviously, their biases can impair their ability to serve their clients well.

The problem is a delicate one, but it is a critically important one and a particular problem for consumer advocates. Everyone wants protection from bad actors. We've all heard stories about accountants who file aggressively because they know the Canada Revenue Agency hasn't historically audited the line item that is being fudged. For better or worse, those professionals likely know they are taking chances. But what about those actors who are not "bad," who are only human? In those cases, the notion of true culpability shifts. What if the bad actors don't know they're bad?

How can we solve problems that we don't even recognize? The answer lies in introspection, humility, and having a genuine desire to gain self-awareness. The time has come for all of us to reflect on our predispositions and actively challenge them, especially where the presumptive "right answers" no longer hold water.

• • •

This book is about something relatively abstract — human behaviour. The title *Bullshift* is a made-up word consisting of two parts, *bull* and *shift*. Most people are at least somewhat familiar with the words *bull* and *bullish*, which are both used to describe finance industry optimists — and in capital markets, there's a strong predisposition to be optimistic. A *bull market* is one in which prices are rising or are expected to rise. The word *shift* is more readily understood. As a noun, it means a slight change in position, direction, or tendency — some form of deflection. The obvious similarity to another more colloquial word is deliberate. What's at issue might be described in a cheeky way, but the outcomes can be tragic. Beliefs, no matter how widely held, are not the same as facts. There are consequences for getting both wrong.

Bullshift is written with investors in mind. It is intended as a frank exploration of how old habits, traditional attitudes, and unwitting predispositions can produce negative results — even though the people who have fallen prey to these almost always want to do the right thing. It is commonly understood that to solve a problem it is first necessary to identify the problem. *Bullshift* is an attempt to help investors and financial advisers identify the problem of unconscious bias and to show them how to overcome it.

Part I

The Interplay Between Behavioural Economics, Financial Advisers, and Retail Investors

Chapter 1

Understanding Advisers
and the Industry

Don't believe everything optimists tell you
If you do, there's a bridge I'd like to sell you

HERE'S A FUN FACT: every chapter of this book has a rhyming couplet at the beginning. That's an example of the *rhyme and reason effect*, which is a cognitive bias that results in a saying being judged as more accurate or truthful when it is rewritten to rhyme. Hey — it worked for Johnnie Cochran, O.J. Simpson's defence lawyer.

• • •

It goes without saying that people don't spend time worrying about things that they are oblivious to. This is a book about a problem that hides in plain sight yet persists because so few people recognize it. For about a generation now, there has been a growing body of evidence that traditional economic assumptions and models are flawed. In these models, people are assumed to be sensible and self-aware. In fact, though, all of us are essentially misguided or biased. Many of our choices seem entirely reasonable, yet they often fail when put to the test in the real world. Despite this, many traditional economists act as though their demonstrably incorrect assumptions are reasonable. People who provide financial advice are similarly blinkered. *Houston, we have a problem!*

Obviously, when financial advice is based on wrong assumptions, the outcomes can be suspect. A paradigm shift is required, and the stakes are high. To date, too few people have recognized the problem. And unrecognized problems are never solved.

Financial goals like improved financial well-being and peace of mind are entirely achievable. We simply need to be more careful when making decisions and to rein in our all-too-human optimism. Doing so may make us feel less comfortable initially, but it will serve us better in the end.

Good financial advisers aim to provide a steady perspective and to give honest and practical advice that is based on empirical data. Unfortunately, throughout their careers, many advisers have internalized modes of thought that impair their ability to realize those objectives. Also, like anyone else, advisers have biases. Advisers are not even remotely immune to them, yet they pay relatively little attention to the impact those biases, if they are even aware of them, may have on the recommendations they make. These self-professed "behavioural coaches" are themselves in need of behavioural coaching. As a result of this situation, investors who rely on well-intended but misguided advisers are at risk — and it is likely that neither the adviser nor the investor realizes it.

To be clear, this book is not about motives, although there will be a need to contextualize these from time to time. Rather, it is about the potential consequences of bias in human decision-making. It is a book for investors. Good intentions are laudable, but they are not sufficient; biased advice, no matter how well-intentioned it is, needs to be corrected — or, at the very least, acknowledged.

There are dozens of biases out there. While we'll look at many of them, the one we'll focus on is *optimism bias*. It is widely regarded as the "good bias," because it is thought to be relatively benign. Daniel Kahneman, the world-renowned sociologist and expert on biases and behaviour, has observed, "If there was a fairy godmother that could grant you one wish for your newborn child, you should absolutely ask for optimism/joy." Not only is optimism seen as a prophylactic against the trials and tribulations in day-to-day life, but it is also seen as something that adds to people's quality of life in general. In the financial world, optimism is what keeps people invested and steadies their resolve when markets get jittery. Optimism is necessary for setting and attaining goals, maintaining a persistent work ethic, and dealing with challenges. In almost all instances, it is an important emotional and psychological support. Optimism is almost always a force for good.

Bullshift is what results when unwanted optimism is injected into a rational discussion — in the resulting narrative, things seem rosier than they really are. It can be found anywhere people are asked to focus on and imagine the future. It is endemic in the financial services industry but is also typically found in other people-facing activities, like politics. There's a lot of Bullshift in politics.

Investors often accept the advice of their advisers not because the logic put forward is so compelling but because it is based on a viewpoint that everyone seems to prefer. People simply want happy explanations to be true and are more likely to act if they buy into the happy ending being promised.

Advisers are often so wedded to their optimistic view of the markets that they may be oblivious to the biased nature of it. Your adviser is the product of an industry with a deep-seated, systemic bias that favours perpetual optimism. It is an entrenched part of finance culture. Just as a fish doesn't know it lives in water because it has never experienced anything different, so too do advisers feel optimistic. Optimism is simply the pre-installed factory default setting. Optimism is generally good for business, and in truth, it is usually good for the investor's portfolio. But not always.

Boxer Mike Tyson famously quipped, "Everyone has a plan until they get punched in the face." Similarly, every investor has a plan until they experience a *bear market*, and good intentions do not necessarily lead to good outcomes. Bullshift is usually the product of "good intentions." To counteract it, it is necessary to "hope for the best, but prepare for the worst." To be clear, people should absolutely set positive goals. It's just that research shows that imagining negative outcomes can lead to better decisions. It's counterintuitive, but the idea here is to "win by not losing." We humans would do

I'M NOT WORRIED — IT'S ALWAYS OPENED IN THE PAST.

well to design procedures and make decisions while actively contemplating worst-case scenarios.

Gabriele Oettingen, a professor at NYU, has shown that we're much more likely to succeed when we imagine failing to reach our positive goals — as compared to merely imagining success. When we identify obstacles, we can do something about them. Sound financial planning should involve thinking ahead and taking into account positive and negative scenarios.

Al Gore has spoken and written about inconvenient truths. The flip side might be called "happy fibs." We live in a wonderful world, but when people suppress realism, rational decision-making suffers. The intent here is to protect you from the unwitting biases your adviser may have.

Too often, investors will unwittingly trade their own ignorance about capital markets for their adviser's biases about those markets. Investors are merely swapping one set of problems for another, so they need to be careful.

An example: when an adviser makes a recommendation about whether it's best to sell or to hold when markets are dropping, it may well be that Bullshift is at play. Before the fact, there is no way to know for sure which option is best. The advice is almost always to "hold" or to "stay the course" or some such thing. That advice is not necessarily objectively right or wrong, but it may be said to be circumstantially right. If everyone else in the same situation "acts rationally" (code for "in a way that economists predict"), then there will be no major sell-off and you'll have saved yourself some considerable trouble. The decision whether to sell or hold is neither right nor wrong by itself; it depends mostly on the behaviour of everyone else who has investments.

It might be said that the rational thing to do is to hold if you think almost everyone will hold and to sell if you think almost everyone else will sell (and to do so before they make that decision). The decision is largely dependent on the behaviour of the other investors who are in the market at the same time and grappling with the same quandary. In either scenario, what plays out is a *self-fulfilling prophecy* of sorts. The implicit lesson here is that "good advice" involves knowing — in advance — how other people are likely to act. That's not reliably possible.

When an investor engages an adviser, it is often because that investor feels ill-equipped to deal with matters of personal finance. As the saying goes, the job is "simple but not easy." The objective distilled down to one sentence might be "to maximize client-specific, risk-adjusted, after-tax, after-cost returns in order to help clients achieve their highest objectives on their terms for reasons that are important to them." Whew! There's a lot going on there. It turns out that, in the end, a lot of what is required to meet the objective involves focus and discipline rather than intelligence.

Many people hire advisers not because they lack the necessary intelligence, but because they do not trust themselves in making important decisions that they are simply too close to. They believe that using a professional adviser is a sensible way to buffer decision-making to save them from themselves. There's a modern narrative that the role of any good adviser includes some amount of behavioural coaching. A professional adviser would help with the following:

o   maintain the discipline of sticking with an investment plan
o   increase the return on investments
o   avoid making emotional rather than rational decisions

These are all good reasons for hiring an adviser. Tellingly, the most impactful statement of the three is likely the third one — the removal of emotion from decision-making — because the first two reasons depend on the third one being true. In fact, it would be nearly impossible for the first two reasons to come to pass were it not for the third.

Behavioural coaching is a value proposition that many advisers trumpet. I believe that they believe they are genuinely adding value. It should be noted, however, that two things need to happen for that to be true. The adviser needs to have a reasonable understanding of *behavioural economics* and the adviser also needs to be able to motivate clients to act based on that knowledge. It sounds easy and everyone claims to be doing it, but in the end, this might simply be a case of "Cool story, bro."

The problem is that advisers, like all of us, are biased in certain ways, and so the advice they offer cannot always be realistically termed "rational." Bullshift is the usual result. Advisers' beliefs and value propositions are open to examination but are seldom examined by investors — mostly because investors feel ill-equipped to do so. The problem is not one of content mastery; it is one of confidence mastery. Advisers, like everybody else, need to be more humble.

The goal of this book is to help you see how much financial industry bias seeps into the advice you get. The influence of that bias is often subtle, so your adviser likely won't even be aware of it. You will need to continually check stories and rationales to test and challenge assumptions. If the elements of good advice can be questioned and the meaning and interpretation of those elements can lead to radically different outcomes depending on what is focused on, then the resulting advice can be questioned, too. Introspection is necessary. Self-awareness is a precondition of progress.

The aim is to help you better understand why some advisers say and do certain things. Too much of what is recommended is presumptive and attitudinal. We need to come to terms with several industry-sanctioned opinions and talking points that are often just financial-service-industry mantras designed years ago to do what is easiest for the industry, not necessarily what is best for the investor. The request here is that you understand the flip side of the advice you receive. The intentions are clearly good. The outcomes are usually good. The problem is that on a few rare occasions, the presumptively good and well-intended advice you receive may not lead to favourable outcomes.

People seldom "meta think," meaning people don't often stop and think about how they think about things. The presumption that your way of assessing things is correct in the first place can lead you astray and cause you problems before you even get started. Hedge fund manager Ray Dalio has suggested that the two biggest barriers to good decision-making are your ego and your blind spots. Together, they make it difficult for you to objectively see what is true about you and your circumstances and to make the best possible decisions by getting the most out of others. I concur.

• • •

Here's a quiz for you. It's about that band from the 1960s — Peter, Paul and Mary:

Paul is single and being watched by Mary. Peter is married and is watching Mary.

My question: Is a married person looking at a single person? Please answer either *Yes, No,* or *Can't say because there's not enough information.*

• • •

We all need to be clear-eyed about the advice business and less naive about motives and practices. Too often, when people don't like facts, they find ways to change the subject to avoid accountability. Ulterior motives, which are not easy to prove, but which exist nonetheless, need to be contemplated. It appears some people in the finance industry are only too willing to ignore certain facts if they do not align with their worldview. Financial advisers are supposed to counsel their clients by looking at and applying both evidence and context. Instead, it seems some unwittingly offer a spin. Advisers, for all their hopefulness and optimism, may be the purveyors of wishful thinking served up with a friendly smile and a reassuringly firm handshake. People in the financial services industry generally make more money when their investors are calm and confident in capital markets, so why not offer calm and confident assurances that everything will be fine? Some people seem disinclined to let the facts get in the way of a good story — this is a form of bias that we'll look at in more detail later. Of course, many of the best stories are works of fiction.

• • •

By the way, the answer to the Peter, Paul and Mary question is *Yes*. While we don't know if Mary is single or married, she has to be one or the other. If she is single, then she is being watched by a married person, Peter. If she is married, then she is watching a single person, Paul. Whatever Mary's marital status is, the answer to the question must be yes. Most people think it is *Can't say*, but if you stop to think more carefully, the answer becomes clear. Most humans don't stop and think like they ought to. We all have blind spots, and those blind spots are also known as biases.

Chapter 2

——

Behavioural Economics and Human Biases

You may tell others logic is our saviour
Only to find things hinge on behaviour

TRADITIONAL ECONOMICS HAS NO TIME FOR BIAS. According to the traditionalists, people are rational, self-interested actors who are capable of quickly and accurately synthesizing information to come up with optimal solutions. Nice in theory, but not even remotely close to how we actually make decisions. We want to believe we're rational, but that's merely a form of *motivated reasoning*. Most decisions are made emotionally and then justified in more conventional ways afterward.

Economics in general and personal finance in particular are social sciences. While it is possible to observe patterns and generalize in both fields, it's not always possible to predict what will happen, because human behaviour plays a fundamental role in how things unfold. Unlike, say, in physics or chemistry, the outcomes are not always predictable or repeatable. Many advisers fail to recognize this key difference. Those misconceptions lead to questionable advice: investors are told that the past performance of a stock provides a good indicator of its future performance; concentrated portfolios are recommended; and the investors are told that little or no attention need be paid to costs. The evidence shows that people frequently do the wrong thing, and yet persist in their questionable conduct.

The central problem is that people giving advice are likely unaware of their own blind spots. Many advisers, including those who are among the best in their field, are giving their clients advice with good intentions, but are unaware that they are relying on misguided assumptions. Underpinning those is their belief in a model of economics, called *classical economics*, that makes false assumptions about human behaviour. A newer, more realistic model, *behavioural economics*, exists, but unfortunately, most in the financial services industry are ignorant of it; or, if they are aware of it, simply ignore the insights it offers. It is vitally important, however, for investors to understand it and to understand how it differs from the economic model that their advisers likely use. So, let's quickly explore the differences.

Classical Economics

Most advisers do things the same way they were taught to do them in their first few years in the business. Until about the turn of the millennium, economics courses taught *classical economic theory*, which is predicated on the assumption that all economic actors behave rationally — that they make rational choices. The word *rational* has a particular meaning here. It doesn't mean sensible, thoughtful, or predictable. Rather, it means calculated, analytical, goal-oriented, and consistent. According to that model, people will seek out and use all available information, determine the probabilities of outcomes, and accurately calculate the costs and benefits of alternatives. Simply put, it assumes people will make smart decisions with their money. This is an *illusion of control*. Due to the belief that they can explain how things ought to work, many who earn their living in economics are overconfident in their ability to apply old-school principles that have largely been called into question.

If we were to distill traditional economics down to a few defining assumptions, they might be as follows:

1. Everything can be optimized (i.e., there is a "best" possible outcome).
2. Consumers exert absolute self-control over their own behaviour.
3. People reliably act in their own self-interest.
4. There is no bias in our beliefs or actions.

Most financial advisers were taught this brand of economics, which seems sensible in theory but has been largely discredited in practice. Since some very bright people helped to develop the classical school of economic theory, it is no wonder that it was taught in introductory economics classes for so long. In those classes, students were taught a brand of economics that (often incorrectly) assumes the following:

o people are rational (i.e., calculating, goal-oriented, analytical, and consistent)
o people and corporations make decisions that maximize utility and profit
o there is an optimal allocation of scarce resources, usually with supply and demand informing choices and opportunity costs
o it is self-evident that people will always do what's best for them personally
o decision-makers can quickly and accurately do the computations required
o decision-makers act independently and have all available information at their disposal
o the perception of what constitutes value is the primary determinant of price
o values influence choices
o markets provide incentives that people respond to
o competitive markets are highly efficient
o market failure may require government intervention

You know the difference between theory and practice, right? In theory there is no difference, but in practice, there is. *Classical economics* talks about how things ought to work in theory. *Behavioural economics* talks about how things work using, you know ... evidence. Many traditional assumptions are reasonable on the surface but are often quite incorrect. Although it was always widely accepted that it would be impossible to calculate certain things precisely, the thinking was that we should all act as though the presumed precision was possible. In short, old-school economists acknowledged that it was unreasonable to expect people to be perfectly rational, but they felt it was reasonable to build models based on the assumption that people *were* perfectly rational, provided that the models yielded useful predictions.

IT'S CALLED MARKET PSYCHOLOGY.

Behavioural Economics

The problem with *classical economics* is that it makes assumptions about human behaviour that simply don't hold up. In fact, people don't always act rationally — people are emotional, and they have biases. Biases spoil the plot because they cause people to make decisions that differ from what would otherwise be considered rational. They exist everywhere, except in the fictional world of rational economic decision-making. Given both the natural tendency toward conformity and the fact that most advisers were trained using traditional paradigms, is it any wonder that most advisers are blissfully unaware of the relatively new discipline of *behavioural economics*? Some of those that are aware of *behavioural economics* dismiss it for a similar reason — the new worldview is a threat to what they know, love, and grew up thinking.

There are dozens of excellent books about *behavioural economics* in general and behavioural finance in particular. These include *Narrative Economics* and *Irrational Exuberance* by Robert Shiller, *Thinking, Fast and Slow* by Daniel Kahneman, and *Misbehaving* by Richard Thaler. Each has the gravitas that comes with having been written by a Nobel laureate.

A small library of highly readable and utterly fascinating *behavioural economics* books is widely available. Dan Ariely of Duke University is perhaps the most celebrated author of such books. They explore the need for broader self-awareness that stems from the sometimes-hilarious aspects of human decision-making. They explain why humans have behavioural quirks and provide numerous examples of what those quirks are and why they exist. I highly recommend that you read one or two of them if you want to learn more about *behavioural economics*. Chances are, your adviser has not read any of them, because most advisers I know still think that their advice should be based solely on such things as earnings, forecasts, and market share for companies and that it's okay to ignore the emotions, attitudes, and behaviours of individuals.

In essence, this book is a more targeted examination of the behavioural considerations that everyday retail clients wanting to make smart decisions with their money need to be aware of — whether consulting an adviser or not.

Financial advisers are human. We all suffer from behavioural quirks. That means you are unwittingly getting biased advice from your adviser if you work with one. What is less certain is the degree to which your adviser is sufficiently self-aware to take steps to rein in those biases and the extent to which you can protect yourself against the harm that those biases might inflict on your investments. *Bullshift* invites everyone to be accountable for their behaviour. If done properly, both parties can benefit.

• • •

Let's look at some behaviours and how they can be understood, As mentioned, in the traditional sciences such as physics and chemistry, things can be calculated with extreme precision. Economics, however, involves a series of interwoven relationships among a whole host of considerations. As such, cause and effect are less easily determined, and it is possible to observe different results even when the same conditions seem to have existed. There are broad, directional causations that can be identified, but results are not always predictable or easily measurable. The concepts described below do not offer certainties the way those in the pure sciences can, but they still provide the best explanations around.

Game Theory

Game theory explores the challenge of anticipating your opponent's next move. It was pioneered by people like John Nash, the fellow portrayed by Russell Crowe in the movie *A Beautiful Mind*. It has two primary strands: co-operative and non-co-operative. With the former, agreements made between actors are enforceable (penalties for non-compliance can be imposed by bodies with legal authority); with the latter, agreements rely on self-enforcement. To see how this works in action you need a bit of pop-culture background.

There was once a British game show called *Golden Balls* that ran for a few seasons in the early 2000s. At the end of each game, contestants could either "split" or "steal" the grand prize. Each player secretly chose a ball with one of those labels. If both chose "split," they would share the prize; if one chose "split" and the other chose "steal," the latter would take the whole prize; if both chose "steal," neither would win anything. The players needed to predict what the other would do. If they co-operated, they both won.

Sometimes, people could win big by deliberately not co-operating. The show offered a clear example of the fact that decisions are not predictable and that different strategies can work or fail as circumstances (such as economic circumstances) or contestants (*market participants*) change.

In markets, if you knew in advance that everyone else would sell, selling early would likely make the most sense ... and if you knew in advance that most people would sit pat, it would make sitting pat a whole lot easier. Alas, predicting the behaviour of someone else is difficult ... and predicting the behaviour of how many people might act is even more difficult.

I suspect that if you asked advisers to explain why they overwhelmingly counsel clients to hold in times of market uncertainty, you'd almost never get a response that refers to social psychology *game theory*. Most advisers would simply say what their bosses and peers have told them to say: "Hang on." The response is rote, not nuanced or circumstantial. There is a big problem with doing what has always been done: things that usually work don't always work. And if you don't consider that the current environment might be exceptional — where the tried and true won't work — why would you recommend doing anything different?

Greater Fool Theory

A related concept is that of the *greater fool*. This concept focuses on pricing; it posits that the price of an object is determined not by its actual value, but by the relative demand of a specific consumer. You succeed by buying high if you're confident you'll be able to sell higher to someone even more (ahem) "motivated."

This calculus results in what some might portray as an unwitting attempt to engage in a kind of collective, financial service industry–wide engineering of investor behaviour. If the industry tells everyone to hold and everyone holds, then holding will have proven to be the right thing to have done under the circumstances. There's an industry mantra that says "buy low; sell high." *Greater fool theory* says there's absolutely nothing wrong with buying high — provided you can find someone to pay an even higher price when the time comes to sell. Toronto real estate in early 2022 comes to mind as a prime example of this mindset in real life.

Nuggets of advice like "Don't sell in panic when markets are dropping" have become part of financial services orthodoxy. It might make sense not to act in panic, but why would it not make sense to sell when markets are dropping? Is there never a situation when doing so is the best option? The problem here is that such advice is based on an unquestioned belief, not on a rational assessment of facts. The industry will point out that successful market timing involves two challenging and independent decisions — when to get out, and when to get back in. My point is not that these things can be done reliably. They can't. My point is that if the advice is the same under all circumstances, then navigating the difficulties "in this market" is a misnomer. The advice is the same in every market. Whatever is going on today will not change the advice you are given. Such advice is impervious to circumstance.

Beliefs are not facts. Nevertheless, almost all advisers — intelligent, educated people who make a living sharing their knowledge — base advice not on facts but on a strong belief in a truism that the financial services industry clings tightly to: staying invested is good for investors — and it usually is. What is less obvious is that it's generally good for the advisory firms, too.

In *greater fool* markets, people overextend themselves using margin and home equity lines of credit to buy more, paying virtually any price for fear of missing out (FOMO). Somewhat prudent investors used to say, "Buy the dip." In a roaring *bull market*, it's more like, "Buy everything." Both perspectives have been lucrative for advisory firms and, in some cases, for their clients. But FOMO comes with risk. People don't resist their own ideas, and if those ideas involve stretching to put more money into the market, who's to stop them? Even a modicum of prudence is out the window when mania takes hold.

• • •

Different strains of adviser (e.g., whether licensed to sell mutual funds or to sell securities) may be subjected to different types of indoctrination, but, since the advice to hold when markets are choppy has nothing to do with the investment vehicles used, we can take it as a universal example. Most questions can't be reliably answered, but most advisers give the same answers to the following, anyway:

o When will (why did) the market start dropping?
o When will the drop end?
o How far will the market drop?
o If no one can reliably know for sure what will happen, why does the industry almost always offer the same counsel when the downward trend begins?
o Is risk minimization given at least the same weight as return maximization?

Prospect Theory

This brings us to *prospect theory* — decision-making that considers the uncertainty of what the future has in store. It is a vital concept for the financial advice business, yet some advisers couldn't explain it if their life depended on it. One of the pioneers in *prospect theory* is the psychologist Daniel Kahneman, who, along with his research partner, Amos Tversky, designed a whole series of experiments that routinely refuted traditional economic assumptions.

For now, let's look at a simple four-quadrant matrix to think about the rationale and consequences of decision-making when the outcome is not obvious, but under two different market conditions. The alternatives are the same, but, in changed circumstances, the outcomes could be quite different. The two simple alternatives are that the market will either stabilize or go up, or that the market will continue to drop. Here are the four quadrants:

I sell; others hold	I sell; others sell
I hold; others hold	I hold; others sell

The first thing to note is that you are not making your decision in a vacuum. It may be that the most rational decision is the one that correctly anticipates what your fellow investors will do, on average. The second thing to note is the likelihood that the average (i.e., "collective") decision is likely to determine the market's direction. In other words, if enough people decide to hold, markets will likely hold up well, and if enough people decide to sell, markets will likely drop. It might be wisest to decide only once there's a consensus. Let's look at the four options in turn under both scenarios.

If markets hold or increase their value, then the "I sell" option is likely to be unhelpful and the "I hold" options are profitable. If markets drop, then the "I sell" options will preserve capital/minimize losses while the "I hold" options allow for those losses to accrue. The important things to realize are that the "correct" decision is not in all cases to hold and that — and this is particularly important — the outcome is likely to depend at least somewhat on what other investors do. Basically, it makes the most sense to hold if others hold and to sell (early, if possible) if others sell.

The financial services industry consistently advises clients to hold. Almost without exception. This looks like a game of chicken to me. If the industry is successful in getting everyone to hold, then everyone is better off (or at least as well off) as a result. On the other hand, if the industry fails to prevent a massive sell-off, there's a clear early-mover advantage for those who bail out early. Advisers try to get everyone to avoid being a chicken, but if the investor really must be a chicken, then it might be best to be a very big chicken at the first opportunity.

Why is the industry so unwavering in its advice to hold? It's orthodoxy. It's just the way we do things around here. The mere fact that the advice seldom changes even as circumstances change can be either comforting or terrifying depending on your perspective.

Some Major Biases

At this point, it might be worthwhile to offer a quick summary of some of the most common behavioural mistakes that have been documented to date. Remember, these are mistakes that are made by essentially everyone. According to Dan Ariely, who discussed the issue in an international bestseller, people are "predictably irrational." In other words, not only do humans make mistakes, but the mental shortcuts (called *heuristics*) and biases that cause those mistakes are so systematic that people will predictably make the same mistakes.

Since the problems repeat, you'd think we'd learn. It seems people who are ignorant of *behavioural economics* are destined to repeat the lessons it ought to teach us. Since the expectations for ordinary investors and financial advisers are different, I'll use unique examples for each. Some of the most prominent behavioural errors include the following:

Overconfidence Bias

Quick definition	Having an unhealthy belief that you're simply better than you are and that outcomes will be fine.
For humans in general	Believing that you're above average in driving ability or intelligence.
For advisers in particular	Believing that you're above average in stock picking and fund picking.

Loss Aversion Bias

Quick definition	Having a dislike of losing money.
For humans in general	Not selling a stinker investment simply because it would crystallize a loss, i.e., "There's still a chance it might come back."
For advisers in particular	Not encouraging a sale even if the investment no longer fits the client's profile or if there are capital losses to be claimed, thus equating selling at a loss with giving bad advice.

Hindsight Bias

Quick definition	Looking back on something with the mistaken belief that you "saw it coming" or otherwise misremembering your thinking.
For humans in general	Remembering only the occasions in which you were right; misremembering your own certainty.
For advisers in particular	Pointing out only the recommendations that worked out best.

Sunk Cost Bias

Quick definition	Doing or not doing something because you have already invested something of consequence (time, money, etc.).
For humans in general	Not leaving an unhappy marriage because of the time and effort already invested.
For advisers in particular	Not changing a recommendation due to changing circumstances for fear of looking silly.

Mental Accounting Bias

Quick definition	Compartmentalizing broad investments for specific purposes.
For humans in general	Looking at the performance of different accounts separately, even though they are all owned by the same beneficial owner to fund retirement.
For advisers in particular	Playing the performance game by pointing to the account or investment that did well as an offset to others that did less well.

Recency Bias

Quick definition	Putting too much emphasis on the recent past, often by assuming the near future will be similar.
For humans in general	Going with whatever "worked last time" whenever a decision is needed, as if the past is a reliable guide to the future.
For advisers in particular	Taking "the trend is your friend" to heart and assuming that the returns for the next quarter or year will be much like the returns from the last quarter.

Availability Bias

Quick definition	Like *recency bias*, this involves putting too much emphasis on information that is readily available.
For humans in general	Making judgments based on what first comes to mind, literally the opposite of careful reflection.
For advisers in particular	When asked for advice by a client, thinking of the last product or security of that kind that you bought.

Status Quo Bias

Quick definition	Having a tendency to resist change.
For humans in general	Taking an "if it ain't broke, don't fix it" approach.
For advisers in particular	Having an unwillingness to consider new products, strategies, or research.

PART I

Endowment Effect

Quick definition	Valuing things more simply because you already own them.
For humans in general	Using the high point of your portfolio as the reference point.
For advisers in particular	Thinking of your practice's asset levels the way clients think of their portfolio values.

Confirmation Bias

Quick definition	Only looking at evidence that supports your pre-existing viewpoint.
For humans in general	Only reading newspaper editorials that you agree with, or following only like-minded people on Twitter or Facebook.
For advisers in particular	Reading only analysts and commentators that share your worldview.

Herding Bias

Quick Definition	Going along with the crowd and giving in to peer pressure.
For humans in general	Ordering red wine because everyone else at the table is drinking red.
For advisers in particular	Using the same products as the other advisers in your office or sharing the same outlook as your peers.

Anchoring Bias

Quick Definition	Allowing a random number or attribute to skew your estimate.
For humans in general	Making assessments based on the order in which you're given options.
For advisers in particular	Failing to pay attention to the fact that the order in which product attributes are presented can influence what is chosen.

The full list of biases is much longer, but the point is that there are many behavioural biases that affect our investment decisions. Even Daniel Kahneman acknowledges that he has them. If one of the true giants of *behavioural economics* insists that biases are a universal element of being human, we probably ought to believe him. Resistance is not only futile; it is also conspicuously self-serving in intent and possibly self-harming in impact. We're all biased. Deal with it.

Kahneman also says optimism is the one bias he would endow people with if he had the choice. Optimism isn't necessarily bad. In fact, it is often very good. The lesson is that it is always present and that it would be useful if we could be more self-aware when going about our lives.

You can be the life of the party if you want to try a few cheeky *behavioural economics* references on your friends. Two of my favourites are "When I look back, I see that I was guilty of acting on *hindsight bias* all the time" and "I showed a lot of *recency bias* in the past little while, but not much before that, so I don't think I'll be doing that again." The impact of biases on decision-making needs to be better understood in general, but it especially needs to be better appreciated by advice-givers and advice-takers.

• • •

PART I

Now that you have a sense of how traditional economics and *behavioural economics* differ and how the financial services industry experiences Bullshift, we can look in more detail at how your adviser thinks and acts. There are likely to be plenty of smiling faces and favourable long-term outlooks when you meet with financial professionals. That's normal. Optimism is the standard outlook for advisers and you should be surprised if you ever encounter anything different. The attitude is mostly genuine, but can be a little bit self-serving, too. Who's to say where the line is drawn? The message is simple: advisers' intentions are good, but the outcomes of their advice are not always ideal. The future is hard to predict, so the admonition is to approach pretty much everything with a positive mental attitude. It usually works. What should you look for when speaking with a prospective adviser?

Chapter 3

The Role of Advisers

People might question adviser directives
The focus should be on client objectives

WHAT IS THE REAL ROLE OF AN ADVISER? Managing portfolios in volatile markets? Managing clients' emotions? Behaviours? Integrated planning? Something else? Advisers offer a range of value propositions and use a wide variety of products and strategies to deliver on them. What's the interplay among those disparate roles — and what are the tradeoffs involved? When considering the performance of advisers, what consideration is given to their biases — both the systemic kind that exist within the industry and the more generic behavioural kind that we all need to grapple with?

Investors often make decisions about whom to work with based on only modest due diligence or on a referral from a friend with a similar incapacity for the discernment of good advice. If their friend had a favourable experience, that may be all that's required — even if that friend's objectives and circumstances are substantially different from their own. And there's the tendency for investors to want to work with someone who offers reassurance and hope — even if they are not supported by anything real.

We all know what it is to be blindsided. It is also possible to be *bright-sided* — a concept that author Barbara Ehrenreich coined to describe the situation of people being bombarded with wildly optimistic, inspirational phrases. Of course, a cheerful outlook does not solve problems. Ehrenreich has noted the negative effects of positive thinking and the reckless optimism that often dominates our mindset. It's a genuine concern.

Given the choice between three potential advisers who recommend a portfolio of 70 percent stocks and 30 percent bonds, many investors simply elect to work with the person who suggests the highest expected rate of return. If the expectations put forward for such a portfolio were 4.5 percent, 6.0 percent, and 7.5 percent, respectively, most people would elect to work with the adviser who was projecting a higher return — as if projecting a higher return would somehow manufacture a situation where that higher return becomes a reality. A projection is not a promise. In most businesses, the phrase "under-promise and over-deliver" is championed. When it comes to financial advice, however, many people choose to work with whoever can set the highest expectation while still seeming plausible.

People quite often respond favourably to someone who offers hope for a better future — especially if that future involves minimal sacrifice in the present. One would think that people who are trying to plan for their future would want to consider the most accurate, reliable sources of information available, but that's not always the case. Learning and applying new concepts can challenge identities and push people out of comfort zones. Telling the truth about the deficiencies of old-school thinking can be bad for business, especially when that business revolves around getting people to buy into an easily attainable future lifestyle or more comfortable retirement. Investors need to guard against rewarding salesmanship over transparent evidence.

In their efforts to persuade investors that they can deliver solid returns and the rosy future they are seeking, advisers sometimes offer up pat advice, as if a one-size-fits-all approach makes sense in every instance. In support of their predictions, advisers will often trot out several well-worn rules of thumb. These include the following:

o The *rule of 72* which supposedly shows that your rate of return divided into seventy-two will give you the number of years it takes to double your money. This can be an accurate tool for estimating portfolio growth, but the factor inputs used are often wildly optimistic.

o The principle "Set a reasonable asset allocation and rebalance annually" has adherents, but they generally pay scant attention to market valuations.

o The recommendation "Buy low; sell high" is perfectly fine in theory, but nearly impossible to follow in practice — especially when the market is highly volatile.

Many of these concepts are staples of the financial advice industry. They are handy proxies for both behaviour and expectations.

Is the advice offered based on catchphrases that are past their due date — or is it professional, evidence-based, and customized to the investor's unique circumstances? If it is evidence-based, just how credible is that evidence, and how familiar is the adviser with it, really?

A man who buys life insurance and ultimately dies while the policy is in place is not so much prescient as responsible and practical. People don't buy insurance because they expect to die prematurely, they buy it to protect their loved ones in case they die prematurely. Buying a life insurance policy is essentially a hedge that responsible people put in place because they feel they must manage the significant financial risk associated with premature death.

People who buy life insurance are being forward-looking and planning for a wide variety of contingencies and outcomes. Thinking ahead, planning for what may or may not come to pass, is just prudent. It has nothing to do with forecasts, predictions, or anticipated death dates. Rather, it's just a strategy for managing risk that implicitly acknowledges that the person buying the insurance does not know what the future holds.

Similarly, taking steps to manage risk in your investment portfolio is unlikely to be an exercise in traditional forecasting, but rather an admission that reliable forecasting isn't possible. If you were the only homeowner in your town who bought property insurance and there was a fire that caused the entire town to burn down, would people ask how you "knew" there would be a fire? Or would they ask everyone else in town why they were so cavalier as to not buy property insurance in the first place?

In the post-Covid-19 world, there was considerable evidence that the market run-up of 2020 and 2021 would not end well. Some advisers did little to manage risk in anticipation of a major drop. Why were these advisers so unconcerned about the risks associated with current circumstances, including (for example) U.S. market valuations that were far higher than in the run-up to the 1929 market crash? Why was there an air of calm when warning signs were flashing?

. . .

A significant portion of traditional financial advice is designed to manage liabilities for the advice-givers, not to manage risk for the recipient. The focus is often on return maximization, not risk minimization. This tendency offers a clear picture of potential adviser bias.

For instance, the concept of *bounded rationality* could be added. It assumes that practical elements such as cognition, energy, and time limitations

THE LAST ONE I DATED WAS LIKE A MUTUAL FUND —
LOW MAINTENANCE EXCEPT FOR THE HIDDEN COSTS.

restrict the rationality of decision-makers. Interestingly, there are two observations that jump out at anyone who examines what most advisers recommend to most of their clients some of the time.

Some advisers are relatively ignorant of much of the best research and evidence regarding capital markets in general. Ask a typical adviser what they think of the efficiency of markets and you are likely to receive a dismissive reply. Any adviser who earns a living on the presumption that markets are inefficient will be biased against evidence of its efficiency. Evidence of efficiency is a direct threat to the value proposition used by many advisers to this day. Being familiar with the concept and the evidence supporting its efficacy ought to be table stakes. In short, some advisers aren't all that evidence-based — especially if the evidence explodes the presumptions embedded in their fundamental value proposition.

It needs to be noted that traditional economics and *behavioural economics* often agree on facts but disagree on the interpretation of those facts — including the prescriptions of how to act and react as circumstances evolve. There's no reason why the two approaches cannot co-exist without conflict. Still, when there are two rival paradigms that hope to explain how the world works, it's just human nature to take sides. As we all know from the polarized and politicized world we live in, people can be all too willing to ignore evidence if it refutes their personal worldview. Tribalism can quickly lead to parking your inquisitiveness at the door to promote your tribe's perspective. Virtually all advisers working today were born and bred into the traditional economics tribe. There's a culture-wars element to advice-giving.

In addition to the tendency toward industry-wide conformity, which is at least somewhat overt, there's the question of adviser susceptibility to the dominant industry narrative, which is a more subtle form of getting advisers to sing from the same hymn book. For instance, how closely do advice-givers watch valuations when deciding about whether their clients should be positioning "risk on" (more equity allocation than was targeted), "risk off" (less equity allocation than target), or market neutral (about the same as the target)? This question is one where fair-minded people might differ.

• • •

There are essentially three primary types of investment advisers:

- those who use micro-level security selection (i.e., they pick stocks)
- those who use macro-level security selection (i.e., they pick funds)
- those who use strategic asset allocation (i.e., they usually mix a combination of passive and factor products, like exchange-traded funds [ETFs] and index funds, but seldom use individual securities or actively managed funds)

The three groups above are not mutually exclusive, and many advisers mix and match both their paradigms and the products used to implement them. Setting insurance-licensed advisers aside for the moment, there are also three primary levels of licensure for investing.

Some recommend primarily securities, some use funds, some use ETFs, and many mix and match the products they use. Some of these might hold a belief in the likelihood that security selection has utility. However, on a balance of probabilities and over a long timeframe, the evidence strongly suggests otherwise.

There is a growing segment of advisers who are both licensed to sell securities and registered as portfolio managers. There are also several related individuals who are registered as investment counsellors, which, for our purposes, means the same thing. The industry lingo uses the two terms almost interchangeably, referring to these people as "ICPMs" (investment counsellors and portfolio managers). These people are obligated to act as a fiduciary when giving advice to retail clients, meaning they must put their clients' interests first when giving advice.

The interplay between one's mindset and one's product registration leads to a fascinating functions-and-relations exercise. Mutual fund registrants cannot recommend securities; but securities registrants can recommend mutual funds. Some securities registrants use mutual funds extensively, but others won't use them at all. Furthermore, there are "wrap" accounts, or separately managed accounts, that are available to all three types of registrants.

These accounts often put more focus on strategic asset allocation, although some use securities, some use ETFs, and some use funds. Some advisers use wrap accounts; some don't. Some use them, but only for certain clients. Most retail investors who are unaware of these variations are setting themselves up for a Forrest Gump–type experience, where "Life is like a box of chocolates — you never know what you're gonna get."

The bias that consumers need to be aware of is one of *licensure*. It is neither good nor bad, but it is real, and people ought to be mindful of it. People have no trouble in recognizing that advisers will only recommend products they are allowed to recommend, yet that obvious consideration is often *not* considered.

On the securities side, there are two primary subcultures: traders and allocators. Traditional stockbrokers are often traders who think they are adding value by trading securities. They aim to go up by more than the market when things are bullish and to go down by less than the market when things are bearish. Unfortunately, there's a small mountain of evidence that their premise (i.e., adding value by trading securities) is unlikely to yield fruit reliably. Either way, it's about security selection, not strategic asset allocation for these folks.

The other culture is that of strategic asset allocators, many of which engage in financial planning. These people understand the research showing a person's strategic asset allocation is the primary determinant of risk and return. Nonetheless, their slavish commitment to not trying to time the market causes them to disregard valuations along the way — even though many of these people would describe themselves as value investors. No matter how high valuations become, the most they will likely do in response is rebalance back to a target mix. They won't even move to be in the conservative end of an accepted range of a target allocation plus or minus 10 percent. If the target mix is 70:30 and markets have gone up and accounts are 75:25 — perhaps because of multiple expansion and ridiculously high valuations — the rebalancing is likely to only go back to 70:30. Not even a tactical underweight is used in most instances.

The premise that asset allocation is of paramount importance essentially requires that no attention be paid to valuations. But even if there's agreement that something is of primary or paramount importance, that doesn't mean other considerations should be ignored altogether.

Of course, like everyone, both groups of people have their biases. Even "enlightened" advisers may still be somewhat blinkered and lacking in intellectual curiosity. The enlightened few are better than the large majority that are misguided because of their obliviousness to evidence, but even the good ones may be misguided because of the precepts they follow. These might include a determination to stay invested at all costs, no matter how much evidence there is from other credible sources that it might be prudent and responsible to divest — at least from a behavioural perspective.

Here's a thought exercise for investors. Consider the following questions. Why do some advisers often hold positive viewpoints on capital markets even when things are challenging? Will these people ever be bearish? What has to happen for their view to change?

To be relentlessly positive is potentially dangerous. The problem, it seems, is that having given that same advice for so long and given that that advice has generally worked out in the past (because *bear markets* have been relatively rare and short-lived), the presumption is that the optimism that has worked in the past is likely to work in the future, too. Not necessarily. Adopting this position opens the door for an *escalation of commitment*, a doubling-down. When you've already taken a certain position on a matter that is turning sour, you can be modestly wrong if you own up now, or spectacularly wrong down the road … but you have only a small chance of being vindicated.

Imagine doctors never acknowledging their patients' sicknesses. Ignoring facts does not make those facts disappear — and there are none as blind as those who do not want to see. Many advisers shift the focus when pressed. The resulting advice is compromised. Being perpetually bullish is obviously not consistent with a dispassionate assessment of things.

• • •

Bullshift thinking has several associated adages. Some that are commonly cited include the following:

o   Don't try to time the market ... or, it's time IN the market; not timING the market.
o   This is a stock picker's market.
o   Just buy and hold — there is no *sell*.

Everyone is entitled to an opinion. Hopefully, we can all agree on something so basic. Once we get past that simple axiom in the age of alternative facts, the problems start. The problem is twofold: determining what is actually true, and then further determining whether that conclusion is a matter of fact or mere opinion. The example that everyone is familiar with is the contested result of the 2020 American presidential election. Both Joe Biden and Donald Trump claim to have won. They cannot both be right, so it would seem this is clearly a matter of fact. However, given that about a hundred million Americans believe Trump won, despite considerable evidence to the contrary, to the public, the question has largely morphed into a matter of opinion. And since everyone agrees that people are entitled to their opinions, the "stolen election" narrative lives on.

We live in a world where *motivated reasoning* is creeping into all manner of decisions. Combined with *confirmation bias*, which is when one looks for evidence, but only as long as it takes to find literally the first shred of it that supports a pre-existing viewpoint, we face important challenges in the search for truth. Specifically, we live in a world where people can't even agree on basic facts to have a meaningful exchange of competing viewpoints, much less come to lasting resolution.

Consider the notion of the *stock picker's market*. On the surface, it seems uncontentious. The term has existed for decades and crops up from time to time in financial newsletters, commentaries, and the like. It is loosely understood to mean a set of circumstances that makes for profitable outcomes for those traders who can capitalize on a situation.

But, as with many things in life, proving it exists can be challenging. People can differ about even this. Is such a market even possible?

I am compelled to believe it is not, by the logic of countervailing outcomes. The yin and yang of life means that a market where stock pickers reliably add value seems a stretch. Whenever a stock is traded, the two stock-picking counterparties cancel each other out. To the extent that one side "wins" the trade, the other side "loses" by the same amount (setting aside transaction charges and tax consequences). I believe this simple, self-evident consequence rises to the level of confidence required to assess the situation as demonstrably factual. There are no exceptions to it.

This elegant element of offsetting outcomes holds true in all environments: inflation; deflation and growth; *bull markets* and *bear markets*; easy money and tight money — you name it. Basically, there is no overarching circumstance where all traders gain an advantage because the environment changes. Therefore, the implied circumstantiality of "entering into" a *stock picker's market* strikes me as highly suspect. Even if stock picking were to be an intellectually consistent value proposition for adding value, it seems to me that it would be one that could be acted on at all times and in all circumstances, not something that could be turned on and off like a light switch.

Financial advisers are only human. They are subject to the exact same tendency to make decisions using rules of thumb, unexplored cognitive biases, and unrecognized personal preferences as anyone else. The problem investors are likely to encounter is that they are expecting someone who is "better than all that" when they hire an adviser. Investors should lower their expectations of what advisers (even the very best ones) can do. Investors expect to work with someone who will offer genuinely customized judgment, but all judgments are constrained by the biases of those who offer them. Besides, people are motivated by the prospect of financial success. Telling them they have no reliable reason to think you can make them do well — or at least better than average — is not exactly the kind of counsel that'll get people to turn over their life's savings.

• • •

In the coming chapters, we'll be exploring how this tendency for advice-givers to be upbeat plays out. The desire to exhibit and even perpetuate a form of positive psychology among investing clients seems stronger than ever, perhaps serving to maintain confidence in the economy as a whole and in capital markets particularly. However, is it appropriate? Since the most obvious case study for adviser conduct in rapidly changing circumstances is that surrounding the joint crises of the Covid-19 pandemic and the subsequent stock market drop, we can examine how the interplay between these two events played out in real time and as new information became available.

There's a massive risk that *recency bias* will be a big problem. The drawdown of about 35 percent that played out over a blink-and-you-miss-it five-week period in February and March of 2020 has almost certainly caused so-called long-term investors to think they'll be able to ride out the next drop, too. Japanese investors are now well over thirty years into the trough following the Nikkei peak of the late 1980s. I strongly doubt all but the most patient North American investors could wait even one-third that long.

Using the recent pandemic experience as an example, it might be useful to ask ourselves about both preferences and relative merit. As investors, should we want advisers to minimize negative consequences and ignore disquieting evidence in the hopes of maintaining a general degree of confidence among the citizenry — or to doggedly point to reliable evidence and historical context while being measured and nuanced in the delivery of facts? We all claim to want the latter, but business practices seem to suggest that we continue to act as though we prefer the former — almost despite ourselves.

Too often, people fall into the easy, self-serving trap of engaging in *motivated reasoning*, where they cease to be dispassionate decision-makers and transform into some sort of stock-market cheerleaders. Wanting things to be fine doesn't make things fine. Reassurances that have no grounding can do more harm than good when it becomes apparent to everyone that they were empty in the first place. Being an optimistic voice of calm may be fine and good most of the time, but doing so while deliberately not looking at the situation in a balanced and realistic way can lead to poor diagnoses of problems and, ultimately, to poor decisions.

Like anyone else, advisers can be marginalized if they take a position that is contrary to the majority groupthink. For instance, the mantra "There is no sell" became culturally ingrained a couple of generations ago. Few have had the courage to challenge it since. Even fewer have successfully done so. You are neither right nor wrong because people agree with your opinion. You are right when the facts support your position and wrong when they do not. Everything else is narrative. The other consideration at play is career risk. That's when being conspicuously unlike your peers, whether through action or inaction, can be bad for your career's trajectory if you turn out to be wrong. If everyone else is wrong with you, that risk is managed.

Too often, people confuse facts and opinions and not everyone has the self-assurance to profess unpopular opinions when others are critical of them. Here's a possible fix: perhaps overly optimistic advisers should frown more. Seriously. Frowning activates the skeptic within us and works to reduce *overconfidence*. It also causes us to be more analytical, more vigilant, to think more deeply, and to question stories that we would otherwise accept simply because they are simple and coherent. The advice business rewards confidence. Confidence requires a firm handshake, a steady gaze, and, yes, even a measured smile from time to time. But such confidence can be unfounded and misleading. If only we could do something about it.

Chapter 4

What Needs to Change?

Why do adviser attitudes last?
Too often, their knowledge is stuck in the past.

WE NEED TO BE CAREFUL not to label errors made in good faith as deliberate manifestations of bad intentions. Investors need to be assured: the very large majority of advisers act in good faith when dealing with the public. That said, it is clear that investment advisers make mistakes and that they have biases — conscious and unconscious. They are, after all, human. While this must be recognized, it is important to not cast aspersions on the well-intended people who may be making entirely human mistakes. No one wants to make mistakes, but we all make them anyway. How do we solve this serious problem without making it look like we're attacking the people who sometimes make mistakes even though they absolutely want to do what's right?

David MacDonald and Robert Stel of Environics Research have looked into adviser attitudes. It turns out that with investment advisers, much as with do-it-yourself investors, a high degree of optimism correlates with a high risk tolerance. The obvious concern here is that some advisers' personal high tolerance for risk might cause them to encourage (or at least allow) certain clients to take on more risk than they otherwise might.

This elevated tolerance for risk is to some degree the result of *overconfidence*. Those advisers are pretty sure they've "got it down" already in terms of what to say and what to do. They are optimistic about their abilities. As well, they find comfort in the fact that most of their peers are saying and doing essentially the same thing (*herding bias*). As individuals, most advisers are beholden to the wider *industry group bias* (also called *in-group favouritism*) that results in people favouring others that are like themselves in terms of values, outlooks, and allocation of resources. According to Warren Buffett, the five most dangerous words in business are "Everybody else is doing it."

When there is an industry-wide consensus on what's best to do, how exactly does one change that? And how do you persuade individual advisers and the financial services industry as a whole that they have biases that may be causing them to give poor advice to their clients? That's our challenge.

No one ever solved a problem that they didn't recognize as a problem in the first place. "If it ain't broke, don't fix it." But the problem is obvious. If you don't recognize that something is "broken," it will never be "fixed." Followed to its logical conclusion, the overly optimistic advice being given by much of the financial services industry is not likely to change if the industry is incapable of acknowledging the inherent biases that have allowed questionable advice to persist until now.

The Dunning-Kruger Effect

A little over twenty years ago, two academics from Cornell, David Dunning and Justin Kruger, released groundbreaking research that showed something that many people had long suspected. This was simultaneously earth-shattering news and non-news, depending on where you stood.

In short, they showed that some people are simply too incompetent to recognize their own incompetence. The phrase "You don't know what you don't know because you don't know what you don't know" had been used extensively before their seminal paper was released, but their work detailed just how true that phrase is.

The way the Dunning-Kruger findings landed depended on several factors — including the innate level of cynicism people might have. Relatively self-aware people tended to receive the research with a collective "Well, duh!" while other, more measured, but less self-aware people sometimes reacted with incredulity. Either way, like it or not, the evidence was clear. Awkward, maybe ... politically incorrect in the eyes of some ... but clear.

If you think you're good at something, but in fact you are below average at it, you suffer from what is called *illusory superiority*. It can be difficult to accept your relative incompetence. Study after study has shown that we all suffer from various forms of *overconfidence*. Way over half the population consider themselves to be above-average drivers. People simply have a hard time accepting their own shortcomings and errors. For instance, the old joke "Once I thought I was wrong ... but I was mistaken."

Kidding aside, very few of the most culpable people recognize themselves in the research. That's because people who are low performers are not only relatively poor at accepting criticism, they also seldom show an interest in self-improvement. In the words of Charles Darwin, "Ignorance more frequently begets confidence than does knowledge."

It goes without saying that this trait is also to be found among investment advisers. They are neither better nor worse than the rest of us. The concern, of course, is that advisers offer counsel to the broader public, and the effect of their counsel (assuming it is followed) affects others in a way that is dangerous. This is a challenge for all of us.

An academic paper titled "The Misguided Beliefs of Financial Advisors" provides copious evidence that many advisers chase past performance, run concentrated positions, and pay little or no attention to product cost. These are all investment strategies that are known to produce less-than-stellar returns — sometimes they can produce losses. The advisers studied would often pursue these strategies with their own portfolios, even after they had retired from the business. They were not giving poor advice because they were conflicted, immoral, or improperly incentivized. They were doing so because they firmly believed it was good advice. They literally didn't know any better.

The challenge for society — and especially for those who receive advice from these well-intentioned advisers — is to find a way to respectfully encourage the industry to address its shortcomings ... and for advisers to raise their game as a result. Alerting advisers to their own deficiencies is a daunting task. How, exactly, might one encourage someone to examine themselves — their beliefs, their level of knowledge — and ultimately change their behaviour if the person who needs to change absolutely believes change is unnecessary? They likely have gotten along fine until now. It's probable that few if any investors have complained about the advice they've been given. In fact, surveys repeatedly show that most people working with an adviser are happy with the advice and attention they receive. Unfortunately, some advisers have become complacent, believing that the advice they provide is based on the best and most up-to-date information available. In fact, some simply haven't kept up with new research and evidence. Traditional economic assumptions and paradigms are being forcefully challenged like never before, but you'd never suspect that if you spoke only to these advisers.

In a Dunning-Kruger world, how does one motivate people who are oblivious to things that they ought to know to learn about those things? There ought to be a fair amount of existential angst in the adviser community, but, because of the widespread lack of awareness about bias, there is relatively little. No one ever became anxious about an inability to answer a few philosophical and existential questions about their professional calling if those questions were never posed, even if only to themselves.

Let's look at this as a matter of principle. If you were giving advice to others, how would you make decisions? Would you focus on the familiar things you know and can do well? Or would you rely more on things that you're less familiar with, even if they have been shown to improve people's lives? It seems that most people will stick with what they know. When you're good with a hammer, everything looks like a nail.

There is no reliable way to completely eradicate the temptations of human nature: take that impracticality as a given and accept it. Issues surrounding conflicts of interest, misappropriated agency, and advisers "going rogue" are both real and troublesome, but that's not what we're talking about here.

Social scientist Herbert Simon showed that most people have good intentions; they aspire to be rational, careful, and deliberative. However, due to the constraints of time, focus, and energy, they tend to "satisfice" — they are satisfied as soon as they encounter an option that is sufficient for their purposes. It seems the industry does little to force deep thinking upon advisers.

Evidence-Based Advisers Also Ignore Evidence

The crux of the problem is that advisers sometimes give bad advice despite having good intentions. They mean well, but because they simply don't pay attention to all the evidence and because they do things as they always have, thinking the rules they were taught to follow remain valid, their advice can sometimes be seriously flawed. They literally have no idea that it could be improved significantly if they were more familiar with developing evidence

in the field. And the unfortunate truth is that even if there were a base level of knowledge about bias in the advisory community, it would likely make very little difference. People have known about the importance of sleep and exercise for generations, yet still we have more sleep-deprived, overweight people around than ever before. Knowledge alone seldom changes behaviour. What's needed is a way to increase advisers' motivation to become better versions of themselves.

Paradigm-shifting financial findings have come to light in the past generation, yet few advisers seem prepared to accept them — although, in fairness, they may not even recognize them. That's dismaying at a minimum and terrifying if fully extended. History is full of examples of the consequences of ignoring — or even minimizing — evidence. It took over a generation for most physicians to "get it" in acknowledging the linkage between cigarette smoke and cancer.

In 1964, when the U.S. surgeon general released the groundbreaking report that provided evidence of the linkage, over 40 percent of Americans were smokers — and fully half of American physicians were smokers. The people who had sworn via their Hippocratic oaths to "do no harm" stood idly by and did next to nothing to disabuse their patients of self-harming behaviour. The parallels are striking. *Motivated reasoning* and *cognitive dissonance* are powerful impediments to progress.

The example above is not an isolated one. Ignaz Semmelweis was a nineteenth-century Hungarian scientist who discovered that if obstetricians washed their hands it would help to minimize puerperal fever and fatalities associated with childbirth. His peers, too proud, self-satisfied, and hubristic to listen, dismissed his findings and had him committed to a mental institution. Here was a great scientist who was ignored and mocked by his fellow scientists because they believed that they were "part of the solution" and couldn't fathom even the possibility that they were "part of the problem." The *Semmelweis reflex* is the term given to the active rejection of new information if it is inconsistent with current beliefs. This reflex can occur even when current beliefs are demonstrably incorrect.

A far more recent example comes from modern times. Li Wenliang was a Chinese ophthalmologist who worked as a physician at Wuhan Central

Hospital. In December 2019, he warned his colleagues about a possible outbreak of an illness that resembled severe acute respiratory syndrome (SARS). Soon afterward, this pathogen was acknowledged as the coronavirus that caused Covid-19. The doctor had tried to warn his superiors and public health officials, but his evidence was initially denied and covered up. Telling the truth can be bad for business.

Once again, we come to a point where we need to at least try to distinguish between conscious bias and unconscious bias. Because of plausible deniability, there may never be a way to know exactly where one ends and the other begins. No matter how widespread unconscious bias may be, however, we should not be naive about the possibility that people will sometimes do bad things, even in full awareness of their own true motives and beliefs.

Wash Your Hands

The stories of Ignaz Semmelweis and Li Wenliang have an interesting thing in common. Both demonstrate the virtue of washing your hands — literally. They also demonstrate how powerful interests can band together to protect their turf, cover up evidence for as long as possible, and wash their hands — figuratively — of all responsibility and consequences once that evidence comes to light.

The individual scientists who might equally be called pioneers or whistleblowers likely weren't seeking fame and fortune. Rather, they simply wanted to do what was right because it was the right thing to do. They were like the Tom Cruise character in the movie *A Few Good Men* who insisted "I want the truth!" while their colleagues were like the Jack Nicholson character, saying, "You can't handle the truth!" It's interesting how the people with the most to lose anoint themselves as arbiters of what people can and cannot handle and what they should and should not know.

There are several things in the financial services industry that are known to be true, but that the industry systematically either denies or changes the subject about when confronted with evidence. Some advisers may not be familiar with these, depending largely on licensure, peer groups, and intellectual curiosity. They include the following:

o Product cost and product performance correlate negatively.
o Products that display outperformance cannot be reliably identified in advance.
o Products that display outperformance after the fact do not persist in doing so more than would be expected by chance.
o The cost of advice should be taken into consideration when doing your planning.

Society has long been aware of the risks associated with accountants who don't keep up with changes in the tax code and physicians who aren't current regarding new treatments and pharmaceuticals. That concern ought to apply to financial professionals, too, yet hardly anyone thinks about advisers who are behind the times regarding evidence — as if "buy low; sell high" is all you need to know. There's more to financial advice than simply recommending the latest whiz-bang product or security. Unfortunately, there are plenty more continuing-education credits associated with products than there are with solid, but generic, facts. Some practitioners claim to know more than they do, fail to keep up, and actively deny anything that is both new and contrary to their preestablished understanding.

It is precisely because the industry makes money by not drawing attention to certain evidence that we have this problem — and it is not easily addressed. The culprits are those advisers who are unaware of their own deficiencies because they accept the primary premise of what adds value (picking stocks or picking someone who will pick stocks for you and your clients) that they don't stop, step back, and truly reflect on whether or not that fundamental premise is, in fact, correct.

The lack of willingness amongst investment advisers to accept new information may be due, at least in part, to the strong desire to do what's best for clients. Once you really, really believe that the fundamental value proposition involves some form of security selection, that belief naturally becomes your primary focus; but the rhetorical questions abound:

o What if those good intentions are precisely what prevent the advisers from offering something better?

o What if the good is the enemy of the best?

o How can we motivate advisers to reconsider their value proposition if they absolutely believe everything is fine as it is?

It may well be that some advisers have convinced themselves that they're already doing a good job. Assuming that's the case, it makes sense that any suggestion to the contrary will be resisted. It comes down to this: When you know in your heart of hearts that your intentions are good, do you ever genuinely question your actions? That's the problem.

Eugene Fama at the University of Chicago (a Nobel laureate, famous for his work on the *efficient-market hypothesis*) is widely referred to as the "father of modern finance." If you were to ask many financial advisers who Fama is, you'd likely get a blank stare. Ask those same advisers what they think or know about Warren Buffett, and they'll go on for hours. The observation is telling. You'd think finance professionals would have at least a passing familiarity with the father of modern finance. Try to imagine a professional psychoanalyst who has never heard of Sigmund Freud.

Some advisers are quite happy to embrace the elements of economics that suit them and to discard those that do not (*confirmation bias*). For instance, fundamental analysis and technical analysis have roots in the rationalism of value investing. It simply makes sense to buy things when they're "on sale." However, as soon as the framework cuts against their presumptive value proposition, advisers choose to look the other way. Fama's evidence, as corroborated semi-annually by Standard and Poor's in every major developed market in the world over three-year, five-year, and ten-year timeframes, shows that most people who try to beat the market fail to do so. The story of stock-picking is a compelling one from the perspective of product sales (and fits with *optimism bias*), but the evidence of wholesale stock-picking failure is irrefutable.

Think about this logically. If two enlightened, fully aware, self-interested stock traders complete a transaction and trade some securities, one of them must be "right" and the other "wrong." The act of trading is not accretive in aggregate. This self-evident vignette is a simple example of overconfidence. The stated value proposition that stock-pickers can reliably "add alpha" (i.e., produce outsized risk-adjusted returns) has been thoroughly discredited. However, some people (including some advisers who may or may not be wilfully ignorant of the evidence) continue to purport to be able to do so because others (i.e., their valued clients) think they can. There's no compelling evidence that people can reliably add value through security selection, but since reliable security selection is a value proposition that still has traction (i.e., lands new clients), those who engage in it do nothing to disabuse their clients of the futility of their pursuit. This is a classic example of outdated thinking in operation.

Fama's hypothesis that markets are highly efficient remains as a sensible starting point. Evidence suggests that they are. Of course, if markets are highly efficient, that makes reliable stock-picking improbable.

That, in turn, brings us to the question of culpability. Some advisers do things (promote ideas, recommend products) because they simply don't know any better and honestly believe they're doing everything right. What about those who certainly know they are engaging in Bullshift, or those who, at a minimum, strongly suspect it? Jason Zweig of the *Wall Street Journal* has suggested there are three approaches to advising:

1. Lie to people who want to be lied to, and you'll get rich.
2. Tell the truth to those who want the truth, and you'll make a living.
3. Tell the truth to those who want to be lied to, and you'll go broke.

The problem of getting advice that is consistent with evidence is an interesting one that almost no one thinks about. Many advisers literally don't know the evidence. A few do, however. If they don't know they're wrong, you can hardly blame advisers' intentions, although you might legitimately ask why they don't know what they ought to. On the other hand, if the adviser in question is one of the ones who know the value proposition is wrong, but recommends it anyway, then there's proof of questionable intent. It leads us to a problem of plausible deniability. Sometimes, it's just easier to claim ignorance than to be accountable for advice.

Unfortunately, even more enlightened advisers who know and understand the evidence and who are also familiar with the more applied concepts championed by the likes of Warren Buffett and John Bogle (the inventor of the first index fund) are nonetheless often prone to give short shrift to the emerging evidence put forward by the upstart behaviouralist school. In fact, many self-professed evidence-based advisers don't really apply *behavioural economics* evidence. Those that know the traditional (presumptively logical) perspective often ignore the equally valid, but less traditional (demonstrably emotional) evidence. That's the thing about evidence — it has no ideology.

Behavioural Economics in Practice

Cherry-picking the evidence that suits your predisposition is a form of *confirmation bias*, and some of these champions of evidence are themselves often guilty of not considering some of the most robust and credible behavioural evidence available.

As it stands today, virtually no one offers financial advice that reflects behavioural concepts. Minimizing the emotional hurt of seeing your portfolio value drop can be a genuine benefit for many retail investors. However, reducing that suffering might involve selling off certain risky positions when markets are fragile. Compensation structures that are asset based may lead to some advisers having a conflict between their interests, their employer's interests, and those of their clients. Furthermore, since economics isn't really a science, but more of a study in human interactions based on conflicting emotions and motives, decisions are likely to be imperfect. We all react differently to challenging circumstances. Playing defence doesn't always pay off.

Similarly, overcoming *present bias* and investing for the long term can create short-term losses that are unappealing, even if they are overcome in the long run. Still, the industry has put powerful incentives in place to get advisers to encourage their clients to stay invested. I'm not saying it's always wrong; I'm saying the industry is disingenuous in implicitly insisting that its position is always right.

That's another problem associated with embedded-compensation mutual funds. Money market funds pay little or no trailing commission, sometimes called "trailers." Trailers are paid directly to the adviser by the fund company. A fund costing 2.4 percent might pay the adviser 1 percent from that. Similarly, one could buy a fund that costs only 1.4 percent, pays the adviser nothing, but then pays the adviser a separate fee. Quantum of pay is similar, but there are differences in transparency and tax treatment.

If advisers recommended embedded-compensation mutual funds to their clients and there were some miraculous way to foresee a massive *bear market* in both stocks and bonds lasting six months (meaning they should ask their clients to move their holdings into money market funds while the storm passes), the advisers would essentially have to pay their expenses while earning virtually no income at all for half a year. Is it really any wonder that advisers are pretty much all permanent bulls?

· · ·

The public's presumption has been that advisers are sufficiently self-reflective regarding their calling that they perform their work with diligence. I have spoken with dozens of advisers who tell me that they find their work highly rewarding — and not just in the financial sense. Many advisers take enormous pride in their work.

Taking pride in challenging and meaningful work is a hallmark of true professionalism. Professionals seek to do the right thing for the right reasons when offering their services to the public, and financial advisers are no exception. There's real honour in aiming to assist people in achieving some of their life's most important goals, provided the work is done with integrity. In short, good advisers need to be authentic. Authenticity is a simple character trait. It is the degree to which one's actions are congruent with one's beliefs and desires. Ideally, this congruency should exist despite external pressures such as the priority-warping temptations itemized earlier.

How well do advisers fit the bill? If you asked most advisers, you'd likely hear them self-assess glowingly. However, we know from David Dunning and Justin Kruger that many of us are prone to blind spots where our competence may be wildly overstated — perhaps because we are unaware of what we could be. The question that it raises, however, is "When does overconfidence give way to incompetence?"

It seems some advisers have fallen prey to presumptive value propositions of stock picking, fund picking, performance chasing, and trend following. Meanwhile, they have often managed money in ways that are less than optimal in their desire to help their clients. Achieving long-term, risk-adjusted, client-specific, after-tax, and after-cost returns involves the following:

o diversifying — both within and throughout asset classes
o minimizing turnover (and associated taxes)
o minimizing costs — both for products and for the services rendered (many employers resist having their advisers speak this truth)
o offering true customization for client needs and circumstances
o adding value through tax integration, estate planning, and financial planning

For now, the big question is "How does one admit to one's clients that one has been overly optimistic?" What kind of angst might be conjured up in making that admission? An attitudinal sea change seems to be needed. Once advisers can be introspective enough that they can be made to see that they have been giving advice without proper consideration of behavioural biases, a wholesale re-education will surely be in order. As is so often the case, the first step in solving a problem is admitting you have one.

How Do Advisers Behave?

Say markets around the world drop by 20 percent. What does the adviser say and do? *Prospect theory* teaches us that the pain of loss is twice as great as the joy of gain. Furthermore, people who sell when markets are dropping need to be right two times: they need to know when to get out and when to get back in — and no one can time markets reliably. If a meaningful part of an adviser's job is to act as a behavioural coach, what should a good, reputable, and enlightened adviser do?

Let's say the TSX is at 20,000 when it begins to drop. What's the narrative at 19,000? 17,000? 15,000? Say a client gets out at 15,000 and the market goes down to 12,500, but then stays out and doesn't get back in until 16,000. Financially, the client suffered a 1,000-point loss that would not have been incurred had they stayed invested. Emotionally, however, the pain stopped when the sell order was placed. We can quantify the financial impact — what about the emotional one?

There's more to consider from Daniel Kahneman. Some advisers would suggest that clients think fast (they are emotional/reactive), whereas they themselves think slow (they are logical/purposeful). Perhaps. That's a good narrative. Robert Shiller's book *Narrative Economics* explores how plausible and compelling stories can backstop behaviours. The recommendation to hold puts a premium on the financial aspect of performance but minimizes the importance of peace of mind. Peace of mind may not show up on a quarterly statement, but clients repeatedly insist that that is the implicit benefit they are seeking when they decide to work with an adviser.

The problem is one of reliable counterfactuals. There's no reliable way to determine the extent (if any) of behaviour modification involved. Advisers want the world to believe that their clients would have done something differently were it not for adviser interventions, but there's really no reliable way to say for sure. Sentences that begin with "stay calm" are potentially offensive if people are calmly telling you to stay invested while your portfolio drops.

It ultimately becomes a game of chicken. The strategy either works (i.e., the client stays invested, and the market eventually surpasses the previous high) or it magnifies the pain (i.e., the client doesn't sell when they want to but loses their nerve and sells when the market is far lower). In the second scenario, it's not just the pain of the loss, but the pain of the opportunity cost of not having gotten out sooner (i.e., when the investor wanted to in the first place). Not only did the client lose money, but the client lost substantially *more* money than they wanted to or were comfortable losing, precisely because they did not sell earlier. Note that if the client sells at any point, the adviser is deemed to have failed. Basically, if the adviser defines their role as keeping clients invested come hell or high water, then a sell order is tantamount to failure. Pop quiz: which is the bigger adviser failure — the client selling when the market is at 16,000 or selling when it is at 14,000? This is not a suggestion that markets can be timed reliably. They cannot. Rather, it is a recognition that the very human emotion of regret is real. Accepting that no one knows what will happen before the fact, how much consideration is truly being given to how the client would react, depending on how things play out?

Every adviser has dozens (perhaps even hundreds) of individually calibrated risk/reward games going on in their practice. Each client has their own personal risk profile and tolerance. These have different trigger points and hot buttons. For instance, imagine two clients — both earning the same amount, same age, same answers on a risk profile questionnaire, but one is an employee, and one is self-employed. One wrinkle could lead to different risk tolerances and potentially massively different risk capacities.

Advisers usually say their job is about numbers/valuations/pricing, but they act as though everything will be fine — "stay calm, this too will pass." Any adviser who is not a portfolio manager who receives a sell order and fails to act on it may think they are helping their client. In fact, they are exercising unauthorized discretion. Such advisers are not heroes; they are in contravention of their obligations to their client.

Compliance departments actively dissuade advisers from exaggerating positive outcomes, but they do very little to discourage advisers from minimizing negative outcomes. Not only advisers, but also strategists, analysts, and corporate commentators. How many newsletters in March of 2020 said something like the following:

o This was both healthy and expected (only applies to the first ~10 percent drop).

o This will "certainly" not lead to a recession (how can anyone know for sure?).

o Markets will likely be much higher this time next year.

o This won't be nearly as bad as the GFC [the Global Financial Crisis] of 2007–2009.

Do you notice the underlying tone of assurance and optimism in the standard commentary? Why is it okay to say, "We think markets will go up 30 percent," but not okay to say, "We think markets will drop by 30 percent"? When you don't know, the only honest answer is to say you don't know. Pretending to know and then being proven conspicuously wrong fails on multiple levels:

1. It may turn out to be wrong and undermines credibility.
2. If not (depending on framing, wording, disclaimers used), it could be, at a minimum, a severe miscalibration of risk, which shows questionable judgment, making future advice and recommendations less credible — a misappropriation of voice.
3. It calls motive into question. Was the advice to hold being given because it was best for the client or because it was best for others?
4. People generally acknowledge that they can't time markets, but they tell people they should sit tight as if they know the pullback will be modest. I find that curious. If you honestly don't know if there will be a pullback, or, if there is one, when it will begin, when it will end, or how deep it will be, then why do you insist on doing nothing to prepare/respond? Death ... taxes ... market corrections ... all are inevitable. No one knows the details, but literally everyone knows they are coming someday.

• • •

Keynes is said to have remarked, "It is better to be conventionally wrong than to be unconventionally right." In this case, the "better" part of acting in a consensus-based manner provides a certain degree of legal immunity. The question is, Are advisers more concerned with client comfort or with conforming to the behaviour of their peer group? After all, who would blame them for their counsel if all their colleagues were doing the same thing? But if an adviser steps away from the consensus and shows what might be called courage, heresy, or simple independent thinking and turns out to be wrong, there's no safety at all.

The media have a role to play, too. During the most severe *bear market* in a generation, the headlines talked about "a place to hide" and "value in a difficult market" and the like. How about "Just sell and stay in cash until this mess is over"? Nope. The presumption that buying things that will go down less, even as pretty much everything is still very conspicuously going down, is somehow "adding value" is just silly. Is it responsible to drive 130 kilometres per hour on a major highway when others are driving 150? How is being less inappropriate somehow still appropriate enough?

Who has the courage to say the emperor has no clothes? Some media outlets and advisers speak, write, and act as though not selling is the presumptively, self-evidently best option. I'm not saying that it definitely *isn't*. I'm saying they are overstating their case that it definitely *is*. Dropping by a lot, but still less than others, is not a badge of honour. Rather, it is a pyrrhic victory in a reverse beauty contest that you should have had the good sense not to enter in the first place.

• • •

How good are you at challenging your own long-held beliefs and, if they are found to be questionable, are you prepared to change your behaviour as a result? This doesn't have to be about finances. Have people ever asked questions that you cannot rationally answer regarding abortion, mixed-race marriage, or mask mandates? Note that you need not be proven to be wrong. It may be enough to challenge beliefs simply because you cannot verify that you are right. If facts are in question, they should be questioned. You should seek to resolve questions that cannot be answered without falling back on answers that cannot be questioned. So should advisers.

For example, advisers who adhere to strategic asset allocation will often say they want equity allocations to replicate market capitalizations around the world, so that, to return to the example above, when Japan represented over 10 percent of the world's stock market capitalization and the Japanese Nikkei 225 was trading at a cyclically adjusted price earnings (CAPE) ratio of about 60 at the end of 1989, they would have advised that you put about 10 percent of your equity holdings into Japanese stocks. The Japanese stock market is still below its 1989 year-end high, yet many advisers refer to themselves as "value investors."

No one would plausibly suggest that the Japanese experience wasn't a bubble. Bubbles occur. The only real questions, therefore, revolve around when they occur, how severe they will be, and how long they will last. Note that "why" isn't really the question, either. Who cares why? If you could reliably know when and for how long the market was going to drop, does it really matter if it happens for the reason(s) set out in narrative A, narrative B, or narrative C? Is buy and hold really the *only* sensible option? I believe there are times when it might not be.

With Covid-19, the media that told people in late February 2020 not to worry collectively changed their tune to "no one could have seen this coming" less than a month later. You can't be permanently bullish and still be viewed as an honest arbiter of market valuations and levels. Just because no one could have seen something like this coming doesn't mean it couldn't come ... or that worrying about the possibility is not justified.

In 2010 Brett Arends wrote a commentary called "The Market Timing Myth." In it, he says, "For years, the investment industry has tried to scare clients into staying fully invested in the stock market at all times, no matter how high stocks go or what's going on in the economy. 'You can't time the market,' they warn. 'Studies show that market timing doesn't work.'"

Missing the top days and missing the bottom days are equally misleading, yet most advisers conspicuously only tell one side of the story — the side where you do way worse if you are out for simply the ten or twenty best days. However, a study by Javier Estrada showed that both points are indeed true.

Given the psychological nature of investor behaviour, what ensues is fear of missing out on the way up and presumptive panic on the way down. Tellingly, virtually no sale when markets are dropping is portrayed as a purposeful, thoughtful, or steely-eyed sell decision. Rather, sells are almost always accompanied with a narrative that involves some reference to panic — as if calm, purposeful, rational selling were impossible.

Skepticism is a questioning attitude or doubt toward items of belief or dogma. It concerns testing for reliability by subjecting the topic to systematic investigation using the scientific method. The aim is to discover empirical evidence for or against and involves suspending judgment until that evidence is provided. Cynicism, in contrast, is an outlook that is scornfully and often habitually negative. I am a skeptic, not a cynic. More precisely, I'm a realist who approaches situations with skepticism. Skeptics can be optimists; cynics cannot be.

Chapter 5

Groupthink Among Advisers

People pretend that they're having their druthers
In fact, they are merely conforming with others

CAN YOU PERSUADE SOMEONE TO like a product simply by telling them that it's popular? Does popularity signify worth or does worth beget popularity? That's the puzzle about the logic jiu-jitsu that goes on in the minds of some people. The importance of persuading people that a perception of reality is reality has become increasingly recognized. Propaganda has become pervasive, and its success has resulted in transformative changes in society. China recognizes its power and now has programs with hundreds of young people training to become social media influencers.

Imagine meeting a proverbial snake oil salesperson in the old West. The salesperson tells you the snake oil is a near-panacea for all manner of ills. A skeptical member of the townsfolk might ask the guy to prove their elixir does what he says it'll do. The sales representative responds, "Of course it works! I just sold four crates of this product in the neighbouring town. If it didn't work, people wouldn't buy it!" Did you see the jiu-jitsu? Instead of claiming that people are buying the product because it works, the sales rep claims that the product works … because people buy it!

Although we seldom admit it, we're all prone to being influenced by others. This influence can be positive, negative, or neutral. What's important is that we recognize that part of being human is that we are capable of being influenced in our thoughts, values, and beliefs. Here are a few facts about the United States and its stock market as of early 2022. As of that time, the United States had the following:

o   5 percent of global population
o   15 percent of global public companies
o   25 percent of global GDP
o   60 percent of global market cap
o   80 percent of average U.S. investor allocation
o   the world's most expensive stock markets

Despite these indicators, which point to a high likelihood that a bubble had formed and that groupthink was a significant contributor to it, almost no one in the financial world would use the word *bubble* to refer to the market at that time. The fact that the average American had 80 percent of their portfolio invested in the U.S. market could equally be used as an example of *home bias* or *herding*.

Groupthink

Way back in the late 1940s, Robert Merton called the tendency to base our personal opinions on what other people are thinking a "self-fulfilling prophecy." Essentially, people tend to like things simply because other people like them. People are a lot like lemmings — they talk about being independent actors who are perfectly capable of thinking for themselves, yet they frequently choose the path of least resistance and simply follow popular opinion.

A *self-fulfilling prophecy* is a prediction that directly or indirectly causes itself to become true, because of positive feedback between belief and behaviour. Merton is credited with describing its structure and consequences. In a seminal article on the subject, Merton defines it in the following terms: "The self-fulfilling prophecy is, in the beginning, a false definition of the situation evoking a new behavior, which makes the original false conception come true."

In other words, a positive or negative prophecy, strongly held belief, or delusion — declared as truth when it is originally false — may sufficiently influence people that their reactions ultimately fulfill the once-false prophecy. Self-fulfilling prophecies have a *confirmation effect*, in which behaviour, influenced by expectations, causes those expectations to come true.

There may not be any societal group that is as uniformly like-minded as financial advisers who earn their living selling embedded compensation mutual funds. Once you get them thinking a certain way, it becomes nearly certain that they will continue to think in that way. Peer pressure creates a powerful incentive toward conformity. To be independent, one needs to step away from what other people are thinking, saying, and doing to truly contemplate evidence on its own merits.

In 1973, a new term entered the lexicon, one that has a decidedly Orwellian character. In that year, Yale psychologist Irving Janis published an essay explaining how a group of intelligent people working together can sometimes arrive at the worst possible answer. He labelled this behaviour "groupthink," and his theory changed the way the world thinks about decision-making.

Janis showed that people in groups often develop a "pattern of concurrence-seeking ... when a 'we' feeling of solidarity is running high." This might dissuade those who organize corporate retreats aimed at team-building from planning them. The more people are beholden to the perceived interests of the overall team, the more they might be inclined to turn off that part of their brain that engages in critical thought.

Janis's participants adhered to group norms and pressures by moving toward uniformity, even when their policy was working badly and had unintended consequences that disturbed the conscience of the members. He was famous for saying, "members consider loyalty to the group the highest form of morality." Professors at business schools might call that "building a corporate culture." Cynics might call it "creating a cult."

Participants in those critical decisions, Janis found, failed to consider the full range of alternatives or to consult experts who could offer different perspectives. They rejected outside information and opinion if it did not support their preferred policy. And the harsher the preferred policy (in other words, the more likely it was to involve moral dilemma), the more eagerly members clung to the consensus. The behavioural term for this is *confirmation bias.*

Confirmation bias is "the tendency to search for, interpret, favour, and recall information in a way that confirms pre-existing beliefs." People display *confirmation bias* when they gather or remember information selectively or when they interpret it in a biased way. Not everyone is willing to admit they are subject to it, but we are all guilty of being influenced by it. The effect is stronger for emotionally charged issues and for deeply entrenched beliefs. It is generally viewed as something that individuals are prone to engage in when looking into things. Rather than looking at information dispassionately, individuals displaying *confirmation bias* look for and rely to an excessive degree on evidence that supports a pre-existing notion and actively avoid or discount any evidence that challenges it. They also tend to interpret ambiguous evidence as supporting their existing position.

This tendency is something that one encounters in financial trade journals, which are constantly running stories and editorials about various industry "debates." In fact, very little is truly debated, as the two sides often make their points while making absolutely no effort to respond to the legitimate counterarguments and concerns of the other side.

The study of *confirmation bias* began many years ago. A series of psychological experiments in the 1960s suggested that people are biased toward confirming their existing beliefs. Later work reinterpreted the results, concluding that people with this bias display a tendency to test ideas in a one-sided way, focusing on one possibility and ignoring alternatives. The bias has been explained as being the result of wishful thinking and the limited human capacity to process information. Another explanation is that people are more inclined to fear the costs of being wrong, rather than investigating in a neutral, scientific way. Even scientists can be prone to *confirmation bias.*

Janis suggested several possible methods that could be used to prevent groupthink, though he cautioned that they were hypothetical and had not been tested. He stated that leaders should strive for careful impartiality when choosing what decision the group should make; that competing teams should be formed to study the same problem; and that "high priority should be given to airing objections and doubts." As time marched on, more and more people began to think about thinking. How people thought. What people thought. Why people thought what they thought — and what to do about it.

One of the symptoms of groupthink is the urge of those guilty of the behaviour to insist that their view is held as a "consensus opinion." Another is the ruthless desire to suppress any evidence that might lead someone to question it. A third is the urge to stereotype and denigrate anyone who dares hold a dissenting view. This systemic intolerance of independent critical thinking sometimes leads people to become involved in irrational and dehumanizing actions against outgroups. Tribalism takes hold. People close ranks, pick sides, dig in their heels, and do all sorts of other cliché-laden things that are synonymous with not really thinking for themselves.

In its most radical form, groupthink can be emblematic of that kind of wholesale abandonment of critical reasoning, but in most cases, it results in nothing more dramatic than banal conformity. Many people will adopt a ready-made belief system, complete with the reasons for supporting it, from others. Groupthink people have not really examined evidence for themselves; instead, they hold a set of opinions that can resemble the kind of "pandering to the bleachers" sloganeering found in religious cults and political parties. Their "reasoning" for their positions is the antithesis of what would be considered thoughtful, objective decision-making.

As the study of groupthink developed, there eventually emerged a subject area called "judgment and decision making," which is one of the most important areas in all of psychology. Daniel Kahneman did groundbreaking research into how and why seemingly rational people make irrational decisions. Fifteen years after Kahneman's Nobel win, the importance of the field was further bolstered when Richard Thaler won the 2017 Nobel prize based on his research into how people can be gently, purposefully, and nonthreateningly "nudged" into making what are likely to be better, more genuinely self-interested decisions through choice architecture. *Behavioural economics* was finally going mainstream.

BROKEN
BROKER'S LOGIC

Much of the behaviouralist work is rooted in the quirky, often humorous, and maddeningly irrational decisions made by individuals who ought to know better. The human brain is supposed to be able to perform a quick, accurate cost/benefit analysis regarding its possessor's own self-interests in most situations. There are now dozens of excellent books on the topic showing that that is simply not the case.

Uncovering quirks offers great fun for iconoclastic academics like Thaler, but for the rest of us, the recognition of the existence of those quirks should serve to prevent us from becoming smug. With apologies to a major bank, we're less rational than we think. If we're going to be serious about overcoming our own entirely human blind spots, we need to confront them head on. The tendency toward groupthink is one of those blind spots. Something not sufficiently emphasized is that groupthink reveals the "secret power" of leaders to influence group decision-making. Not surprisingly, that tendency becomes even stronger when the leader suggests that everybody must be a team player.

Blind-Spot Bias

Investors are caught in a tough spot. How can an investor discuss with their adviser the latter's bias when neither the investor nor the adviser can reliably discern their own bias? One of the biggest reasons why advisers need to guard against the laundry list of biases described earlier is the catch-all problem of *blind-spot bias*. People fail to recognize their own cognitive biases. Again, everyone is biased in some way or another. Interestingly, research shows we're better at recognizing other people's biases than we are at recognizing our own. Sometimes, we're just too close to situations to see the proverbial forest for the trees. Follow the logic:

o   everyone is biased in some way; and
o   everyone is blinkered in their inability to recognize this; so
o   every adviser (being merely human) is unwittingly giving biased advice.

Investors are at risk. To make matters worse, advisers are unlikely to try to deal with this problem, because of *choice-supportive bias* — the tendency to feel confident about the quality of a decision once it is made, even if it has demonstrable flaws. It's human to defend your decisions, because no one likes to admit they are wrong. You won't have to worry about fixing any biases that you refuse to acknowledge in the first place.

Cognitive Dissonance

Cognitive dissonance is the term given to the mental discomfort experienced by a person who simultaneously holds two or more contradictory beliefs, ideas, or values. This is a consequence of a person's performing an action that goes against personal beliefs, ideals, and values, and occurs when that person is confronted with new information that contradicts their pre-existing beliefs, ideals, and values. Stated differently, part of why many people have blind spots is that there are places they simply don't want to look.

Leon Festinger proposed that human beings strive for internal psychological consistency so that they can function mentally in the real world. A person who experiences internal inconsistency tends to become psychologically uncomfortable and is motivated to reduce the *cognitive dissonance*. This is often done by making changes to justify choices that seem inconsistent and are motivated by the reduction of what would otherwise be moral conflicts. People invested in a given outlook will — when confronted with evidence that challenges their worldview — expend great effort to justify retaining it.

Enabling

Helping others is a good thing. Giving assistance is a good thing. Enabling others is a good thing. Or is it? In psychotherapy and mental health, the term *enabling* can have a positive sense, empowering individuals; or a negative sense, encouraging dysfunctional behaviour. Enabling can perpetuate or exacerbate a problem.

Quite possibly the worst thing advisers can do is to tilt their advice so that it supports whatever they think their client wants to believe. This isn't really giving advice at all; it is simply being malleable enough to give clients what they want. For instance, a financial-decision enabler might set expectations about a high rate of return when trying to land an account, without drawing enough attention to the risks and limitations associated with certain products and strategies. Such an adviser might also take on a significant number of unsolicited orders.

According to Morgan Housel of the Collaborative Fund, inappropriate investing behaviour "is inborn, varies by person, is hard to measure and changes over time." Furthermore, Housel goes on to say, "People are prone to deny its existence, especially when describing themselves."

Missing the Point

There are magazines that are distributed to financial advisers that focus on industry news and practice management. Editorials and comments abound about the value of financial advice. Many of these are simplistic to the point of being misleading. As you might imagine, any publication that caters to financial advisers will have a decidedly pro-adviser editorial perspective. That's all fine and well, but some observers worry about the soundness of the financial advice given considering the echo chamber that many advisers seem to live in. There is a distinction between good advice and bad advice. The distinction is admittedly subjective, but the media don't ever seem to discuss how it is possible to distinguish between the two. Surely to goodness, not all advice is good advice and not all advisers are good advisers. I believe the short shrift given this issue stems from the fact that a more comprehensive discussion of it might be awkward for certain elements of the industry.

Let's begin by looking at the touchy subject of what constitutes good advice in the first place. Obviously, there is no single best set of answers to this question. However, that doesn't mean that there aren't some bits of advice that are generally better than others.

Advisers can serve as behavioural coaches — helping people to save more, to avoid missing deadlines, and to maintain the focus and discipline that might otherwise be missing if they invested on their own. What if the adviser fails to do so? Does anyone doubt that there are some advisers out there who might not encourage appropriate saving or who might not remind clients of looming deadlines — or who might exacerbate emotional, knee-jerk buy-and-sell decisions? Why don't the financial media do more to shine light on those advisers who fail to do those things? I don't even know of a word or phrase that would succinctly describe that sort of behaviour, but it's pretty much the opposite of generally accepted industry-wide best practices.

Similarly, there have been countless articles about the cost of advice, the value of advice, the possibility of a so-called advice gap, and numerous other variations on the theme of how much advisers are paid. All else being equal, low-cost products are preferred over high-cost products — just as a lower-price car or toaster or dress shirt would be preferred if there was a view that the overall quality and all other relevant attributes were otherwise interchangeable. Stated differently, in a world where investment products are commodities, the lowest-cost product is often the highest-value product.

What's Truth Got to Do with It?

Many of us know a few top-of-mind quotes because they are used so frequently and have nearly universal applications. We sometimes trot these quotes out to sound worldly and informed; sometimes we use them to give the impression that we are a bit cynical about the statements others make, since we know how the world really works. The funny thing about personal finance is that many people are aware of many of these old chestnuts and may see the wisdom in them yet are unable to see themselves in the messages they convey.

Mark Twain offered some wonderful insight into why this might be. He is reported to have once said that it's easier to fool people than it is to convince them they've been fooled. I concur. No one likes to be taken for a fool. Furthermore, when one is taken in, no one wants to admit it. Pointing it out seldom solves the problem and often only makes things worse. Next time you come across someone who has been fooled, point it out to them and see how they react. My guess is that the more clearly you demonstrate your point, the more the person who has been duped will resent you for showing them where and how they were taken. It is entirely possible that your duped friend might be more upset with you for pointing it out than they are with the person who duped them in the first place. A debriefing in the name of transparency would be a bit like a magician showing how a trick works. Some things are better left unsaid.

It's bad enough when someone else dupes you. Now, imagine how depressing it would be if you learned that you unwittingly duped yourself. Cognitive biases are everywhere. All of us use various forms of mental shortcuts, thinking we know things that we don't. We make bad decisions based on what we believe to be sound principles and then later find out that we were wrong. All too often, we are uncomfortable in admitting our own culpability.

Over the past couple of decades, the assumption that humans act rationally and in their own self-interest has been shown time and again to be overly optimistic. It's a reasonable and sensible assumption — on the surface. It's just not particularly helpful in practice.

A small mountain of evidence has been put forward by academics like Duke University's Dan Ariely that shows people are consistently and predictably irrational. It is becoming increasingly clear that people do not make investing and personal finance decisions based on a study of finance. Rather, people usually make financial decisions based on the competing options they are presented with. How exactly does one measure (let alone teach) something as imprecise, yet consequential, as financial decision-making?

The Bias Caused by Embedded Commissions

This brings us to an awkward exception. Although so many biases are unconscious and therefore largely forgivable, there are clear examples where the real culprit is self-interest. In those instances, it would be unfair to let the perpetrators off the hook. Sometimes the bias is not unconscious. Sometimes people know — or at least strongly suspect — that there are clear motives for doing certain things. The problem is plausible deniability. How can anyone reliably prove that *self-serving bias* is not unconscious?

People respond to incentives and embedded compensation (specifically, trailing commissions as offered through mutual funds) is a clear incentive. Making clear how advisers are compensated will not necessarily do anything to change the cost of advice, but it can go a long way toward helping consumers make smart decisions. The industry has made a big deal out of opposing how advisers are paid, but that is just a smokescreen to divert attention from the real issue, which is how much advisers are paid. Four quarters do not cost more than a dollar — and not liking having to pay separately for something does nothing to change the quantum of payment.

Despite this, there are still industry stakeholders that continue to suggest that transparent advice is somehow less accessible to investors of all account sizes if compensation is not in the form of embedded commissions — even if the cost of advice is unchanged. Unsurprisingly, advisers who are paid this way are nearly universal in their defence of their preferred business model. They use groupthink logic to defend what they prefer rather than examine evidence about what is best for their clients.

It doesn't need to be this way. The reason for the disconnect is that many consumers don't understand how much they are paying for both products and advice and, as a result, can be persuaded by industry Bullshift to believe everything is fine as it is. Investors elsewhere in the world have benefitted when embedded commissions are eliminated. Doing so leads to better investor protection, better financial literacy, and a clear substitution effect — low-cost products can be and often are selected to replace expensive ones.

Disclosure Doesn't Work

There is a growing body of evidence that disclosure doesn't work the way we think it should. In fact, it often backfires. When the evidence came to light, many people had to rethink their advice regarding what the industry should be doing. What the world needs is something called *disintermediation*. *Disintermediation* involves paying fees separately and getting rid of embedded commissions. Parts and labour sold separately.

The problem is this: once a client has received a disclosure, they often figure, "Oh, this guy is trustworthy … they told me all the important stuff that I ought to know, so, yeah … I'll go ahead with their recommendation." That's a big mistake. There are some huge agency issues associated with the false sense of security that comes with having the person you're dealing with tell you their conflicts and incentives. In fact, many people are *more* likely to buy high-cost and proprietary products once their adviser tells them they cost more or will make more money for the adviser, for their firm, or for both.

If transparency really is an industry objective, wouldn't it be better to have itemized year-end statements covering both the cost of advice and the cost of products? Investors are paying for both; why is the industry only disclosing one? Product cost matters and should be actively disclosed. This brings us to the line of reasoning that I hear most often: ordinary Canadians either "cannot afford" to pay separately for advice, or, at any rate, they "will not" pay separately for it. This is simply untrue.

Changing how you pay for advice does not, of and by itself, change how much you pay for advice. Let's say you went to the company vending machine in the lunchroom to buy a pop, only to find that the vending machine no longer takes loonies. Now, if you want a one-dollar pop, you'll have to plug in four quarters. That's what we're talking about in changing adviser compensation. It is a simple exercise in changing how advisers are paid, but not necessarily changing how much they are paid. There's no good reason to be upset about the "how" as long as the "how much" is the same.

Stop Reassuring People with Empty Stories

Almost everyone likes a good story. The financial advice industry has taken it upon itself to offer reassurances as a standard bromide. Too often, people who give advice to retail clients are so determined to keep those clients calm that they write and say things that they have no way of reliably substantiating.

I have a friend at another firm who wrote a newsletter in early March 2020 assuring readers that the Covid-19 pandemic would certainly not cause a global recession. It did. In fact, only a few days later, economists, analysts, and commentators the world over acknowledged that a recession was all but inevitable. If you don't know, you should just say you don't know. No more Bullshift.

. . .

Since it may be difficult for non-experts to reliably distinguish between advice based on objective, realistic analysis and advice based on groupthink that is informed by self-serving narratives, I'll just ask that you not be naive. Many biases are legitimate and universal. Sometimes, however, behaviour that seems benign and defensible at first might involve considerations that escape your radar. That ability to avoid meaningful detection makes certain conduct tempting — especially if the person, if challenged, can just claim that it was all due to an unconscious bias.

Part II

Applying What We Know to How the World Operates ... and How It Ought To

Chapter 6

Misguided and Human

Advisers and pundits are presumptively pious
They seldom admit that they, too, have bias

HERBERT SIMON WAS A PIONEER in the field of decision-making. (It's funny … I used to think I was indecisive, but now I'm not so sure.) According to him, good decisions should be both correct and efficient — right and easy. Also, decisions must be practical. You need to be able to implement them using a set of coordinated means. Simon coined a couple of terms you can use to impress your friends: *bounded rationality* and *satisficing*. Basically, he said people are limited and lazy, and, as a result, they make quick, imperfect decisions once they have done enough to satisfy themselves that they understand the situation well enough to decide. Doing the bare minimum is enough for most people because they can't be bothered to do any more than that. Besides, it seldom makes a big difference.

To make sense of what comes next, let's take a moment to summarize Simon's two terms. *Satisficing* combines two distinct concepts: satisfying and sufficing. Simply put, satisficing is a form of *confirmation bias* where the decision-maker is satisfied with any solution that seems good enough. Conversely, *bounded rationality* suggests that there are limits to how rational we really are and just how far we are prepared to go in search of truth. For many of us, that's not very far. It is a fundamentally human condition.

To state the obvious: we are all susceptible to making mistakes because of decision-making short-cuts — *heuristics*.

Richard Thaler is a modern-day disciple of Simon's. He often makes fun of traditional economic assumptions and calls the imaginary people in their models "econs" (since no one acts the way traditional economists assume they will act). The traditional model of decision-making portrays humans as consistently rational, narrowly self-interested beings who pursue their interests in the best way possible. Here's the catch: these supposedly "reasonable" assumptions can't always be reliably demonstrated. People are assumed to make sense, but they often don't, because humans are simply not as sensible as they think they are.

It gets worse. When the traditional assumptions are questioned, classical economists simply shrug and insist that they believe the assumptions are useful in making predictions anyway. The assumptions have been accepted as being both reasonable and useful by the economists who continue to use them. Is it reasonable to continue to use models without adapting them if they don't conform to historical testing?

Behavioural economists have demonstrated time and again that people do not behave as traditional economists assume they will. The traditional guys are annoyed with the behavioural guys because the behavioural guys are engaging in what amounts to intellectual guerilla warfare. They're constantly lying in the weeds and poking holes in the traditionalists' theories. The best the old school guys can do is gripe that the behaviouralists don't have a "unifying theory" of their own — at least not one that goes beyond "your traditional theories are way too easy to refute with facts."

Some traditional economists, such as Milton Friedman, have suggested that we should all think and act as if people were like Thaler's econs, with the words "as if" inserted to explain expected behaviour. In other words, Freidman conceded that people are not reliably rational, but nonetheless said it would be reasonable for economists to build models as if they were. Acting and assuming that there is no problem does absolutely nothing to make the problem go away.

Decision-making is the process of identifying and choosing alternatives based on the values, preferences, and beliefs of the decision-maker. We

all make multiple decisions every day: should I order the fruit cup, order the cream pie, or skip dessert altogether? We all need to acknowledge that choices have consequences. What is less obvious is that since we all make so many choices, we might forget we have options in the first place when we fall into routines and follow habits. We do things now because that's the way we've always done things. Like the band Rush says in "Freewill," you've made a choice even when you do nothing.

The best way to minimize human errors may be to set behaviours at a good level and then move on. That's called a default option. The failure to cancel your subscription to a cable network that you stop using after a while obviously costs you money you don't need to spend; however, some defaults can be good for you. How many people can walk into a bar or restaurant only to have their regular server ask, "The usual?" when taking their order? Too often, we simply do what is easy or familiar or both when presented with alternatives. This is a classic example of choice architecture. How options are presented often has a big impact on which option is chosen.

Isn't it reasonable to expect that we might get different results if people stopped occasionally to consider their options? When it comes to how people think, industry Bullshift makes it hard to talk about a course of action that involves the mere possibility of markets dropping in a big way and for a long time because the default option is what is usually presented. The default outlook on life for some advisers seems to be permanently rosy, no matter what's going on.

Investment SIFs

A lot of what is seen as good decision-making is just conventional decision-making. The financial advice industry tends to do things the way they have always been done. Not surprisingly, most advice still uses the same sorts of assumptions that the traditional economists use and spurns the lessons of the behaviouralists. Humans are creatures of habit. Financial advisers are human. As such, they often default to offering advice based on what are essentially their pre-set preferences.

Combining multiple disciplines (especially science and the humanities) is a concept called *consilience*. Use the word to impress your friends. For instance, Richard Thaler's research bridges a gap between economics and psychology. Too often, experts and practitioners in one field pay little or no attention to the findings of another field. Economists tend to think of their work as being based on facts, even though much of it involves directional causation that falls short of certainty. Many people in finance have *physics envy*.

Thaler has developed a growing list of examples of things that theoretically should not matter, yet do. He calls these things *supposedly irrelevant factors* (SIFs). The interesting thing about SIFs is that traditional economists ignore them — even though evidence shows that these things really do matter. Traditional advice-givers make the same mistake. Economists might call these SIFs anomalies, since they clearly contradict what traditional models predict. The thing is, the more examples that are found of instances where the model doesn't work, the more the model itself is called into question. Depending on whom you speak with, some purported investing SIFs might include the following:

o **Past performance of mutual funds.** The research is emphatic that past performance is of no value in projecting future outcomes. Despite this, many advisers recommend products based on their past performance. Why is that? The answer, of course, is because there are still many investors who think past performance does matter … and advisers do nothing to disabuse them of it. There are only two possible explanations here, but I'm not sure which is worse. Either advisers believe past performance matters, or they do not. If they believe it matters, we all need to recognize that that belief has been clearly and repeatedly debunked in the past. If advisers don't believe it matters, why are they still using it to make product recommendations? When advisers recommend products based on past performance, are they ignorant of the evidence, or callously exploiting pre-existing biases? Note that it cannot possibly be neither. Both are awful.

o *Rational choice theory.* This is a framework for understanding and often modelling social and economic behaviour. The premise is that aggregate social behaviour results from the behaviour of individual actors, each of whom is making individual decisions. If you think a stock is cheap and trust your own judgment, it shouldn't matter what others think. Then again, if everyone you know starts selling that stock, it could easily begin to impact performance … and ultimately, your decision. Does what other people think matter? Usually, it does. The term *mimetic optimism* is used to describe the actions of people who want what others have and naively think that a product must be good if other people are buying it. "Social proof" is just aping others' behaviour.

o **Cost.** Note that this applies to both products and advice, but that not everyone is guilty. According to some, cost is immaterial. I have personally heard more than a few people say something like, "It doesn't matter what the product costs; what matters is your net return (after costs have been paid)." When I hear that, I like to ask them to clarify. It seems this belief is largely circumstantial. As for the cost of advice, it is necessary to subtract costs when writing financial plans. In other words, a portfolio with an expected return of 5 percent before costs, but with 1.5 percent in product and advisory costs, should be assumed to return only 3.5 percent. Anything more contravenes international financial planning best-practice guidelines. More on this later.

o **Previous highs.** Reference points in *prospect theory* are the milestones where people psychologically keep score. In theory, it should not matter to a forward-looking investor with a long time horizon whether their portfolio was once 15 percent higher than it is today or not. Despite this, there are many people who "keep score" based on the psychological impact of what could have been — the value of their portfolios at their high points.

o **Experience (or lack thereof).** In very early 2020, no one seemed to be truly afraid of the coronavirus, but who among us really had any experience with pathogens that could cause global pandemics? It turns out that there are considerable similarities between how diseases spread, according to public health modelling, and how a *bear market* contagion might set in.

o ***Sunk costs.*** If you have tickets to an outdoor concert and it begins to rain, would you stay if the tickets cost $40 each? What if they cost $400 each? In theory, the price of the ticket should have no bearing on whether you stay or leave.

o **Dividend rates.** Setting taxes aside, what matters in investing is total return, not how that return is achieved. Therefore, for government-sponsored registered accounts, a company's dividend policy ought to be irrelevant. Merton Miller and Franco Modigliani have proven it. Their theorem shows that the market value of a company is correctly calculated as the present value of its future earnings and its underlying assets and is independent of its capital structure. This is often called the *capital structure irrelevance principle*. Long-term investors should concern themselves with the total returns of their investments, not the way those returns are realized. Two otherwise identical companies should earn the same long-term return if one pays a dividend and the other does not. The growth of the non-dividend company would simply exceed the growth of the dividend company by the amount of the dividend.

Most people don't think much about the supposedly irrelevant factors noted above. Despite this, the evidence has shown repeatedly that, in fact, these things often matter a great deal. *Classical economics* would have us believe SIFs don't exist and that rational decisions can be and usually are made without giving a moment's consideration to SIFs. In contrast, *behavioural economics* matters because it is an essential tool for decision-making. Most advisers have little or no awareness of the field or how to apply its lessons. Investors should be alarmed.

Basically, the entire field of *behavioural economics* is one giant SIF. Many advisers act as though investor behaviour is irrelevant and give their advice as if behaviour doesn't matter — even as they purport to be behavioural coaches! In fact, behaviour has now been widely recognized as a highly relevant factor in investor performance. Pretending something doesn't matter won't cause that thing to not matter.

PART II

DALBAR QAIB

A report called the *Quantitative Analysis of Investor Behavior* (*QAIB*) is released annually by the consulting firm DALBAR. According to these studies, the evidence shows that, year after year, the typical investor in equity mutual funds has only gotten about a 4 percent annual return. Markets generally do much better than that, of course, but the DALBAR distinction is between investment performance and investor behaviour. The clear message is that questionable behaviour leads to sub-optimal outcomes.

The implicit DALBAR message is powerful, but unsubstantiated. I have asked their representatives for a breakdown between the performance of investors with advisers and investors without. DALBAR says the research does not offer that degree of granularity. Hopefully, you can see the problem here.

In my view, the annual report could also be called the "Quantitative Analysis of Adviser Behavior" (QAAB), since many investors work with advisers. Alas, there's no reliable way to untangle investor behaviour from adviser behaviour. The research simply looks at all mutual fund investors; it doesn't distinguish between DIY investors and those with an adviser. In other words, we can't reliably determine how much of the poor performance is due to advisers' advice and decisions. What is indisputable is that bad behaviour leads to bad outcomes. People can't help but fiddle with their money. The old saying is that your portfolio is a like a bar of soap — the more you touch it, the smaller it gets.

Note that the nominal return is the rate of return on an investment without adjusting for inflation. Inflation over the timeframe studied has typically averaged about 2 percent a year. So, in general terms, what we get as a result year after year after year is

- o 4 percent average annual return (this is called "nominal return"),
- o minus 2 percent average annual inflation, equals
- o 2 percent average annual real return (what you get after backing out inflation).

Would you knowingly put your life's savings at risk for such a paltry annual return? Most people likely wouldn't do it. Many investors have done shockingly poorly over the past quarter century or so. The annual studies account for the average fees and expenses paid, but do not account for taxes. In other words, the actual after-tax experience is certain to be worse still.

DALBAR is not alone. Other firms' reports, like Russell's annual *Value of an Adviser* "research" and Vanguard's *Adviser's Alpha* "research," are designed to convince advisers that they are great at what they do. Once again, I need to be emphatically clear here. I'm an adviser. I believe I do good and important work and I believe my peers do good and important work, too. I just don't want to have to endure such insufferable Bullshift.

· · ·

Earlier, I mentioned something called *heuristics*. These are short-cuts that are often used to form judgments, make snap decisions, and come up with easy solutions to what might be complex problems. This happens when an individual focuses only on the most relevant aspects of a problem or situation and draws on previous experiences to formulate a solution.

Kahneman says that since the beginning of civilization, humans have been programmed to make snap decisions — some of which may have even had life-or-death consequences. This is "thinking fast." As time has gone on, however, humans have evolved to become more purposeful in their concerns and complex in their decision-making. Complex decisions require more deliberate thinking — something that needs to be done slowly and methodically to be done well. We have spent thousands of years thinking fast. It's a hard habit to break.

Meanwhile, decision-making these days (such as how to react with stoicism when the stock market begins to tumble) is a modern problem that our ancient brains have been slow to adapt to. Whether we like it or not, we need to learn to think more slowly. It's not comfortable, and, in many ways, it's not even natural, but society demands that we do it anyway.

We are often influenced by our past experiences in our decision-making. If something worked out the last time we tried it, we're more likely to do it again. Accordingly, there are many *heuristics* that can be tailored to solve various problems in everything from psychology to technology design to economics. These processes include those that deal with availability, representativeness, and anchoring. The good news is that, in keeping with experience, heuristic processes and the resulting decisions are often more or less right. Even when they're wrong, the consequences are usually minor — like picking a wine based on the nice label and not liking it. The point is that the fast decisions are not always right. It is simply human nature to do what is easy. People sometimes justify doing things the easy way because doing them that way has worked out in the past. The past is not prologue, however.

Heuristic processes can easily be confused with the lack of use of logic and probability. That confusion misses the distinction between risk (knowing that something can go wrong) and uncertainty (not knowing what the future might hold). Stated differently, risk refers to situations where all possible outcomes are known and considered, while uncertainty refers to situations where pieces of information are unknown. That distinction can have massive consequences.

Behavioural Finance (Not) in Practice

Most people don't give much thought to the biases they have and the implications that flow from them. Then again, most people don't earn a living by giving advice to others when the stakes are their clients' life savings. How much consideration is given to personal cognitive biases that might be held by those who offer advice to retail clients? Here are some useful questions that we can all ask ourselves:

- o Am I chasing some sort of past performance, be it a sector, product, or trend? (*Herding*)
- o Have I thought about other viewpoints? (*Confirmation bias*)
- o Am I avoiding a sale simply to avoid realizing a loss? (*Loss aversion*)

o Do I believe that the market has gotten the price of a security wrong? (*Overconfidence*)

o Do I use plausible, yet suspect stories to explain market movements? (*Narrative fallacy*)

Good decision-making requires calm, purposeful self-awareness and introspection. Perhaps we should all spend more time meditating and being mindful. It seems the opportunities to shoehorn semi-empirical explanations into market gyrations are boundless. For instance, advisers are often blinded by their own due diligence. They think, *If I just analyze this security more than anyone else, I'll have a better sense of its true value.*

Meanwhile, they sometimes use their analysis the way a drunkard uses a streetlight — more for support than for illumination. It should come as no surprise, therefore, that well-intended recommendations often end up being wrong simply because the person making them was unwittingly focused on the wrong things. What could possibly go wrong when self-professed "behavioural coaches" aren't even aware of their own biased behaviour, yet expect to add value? Some advisers even go so far as to suggest that one specific tangible difference that separates them from less enlightened advisers is their ability to constructively modify their clients' collective behaviour.

Let's look at a few widely accepted elements of *behavioural economics* that are often overlooked. First and foremost is *prospect theory*. Advisers seldom apply it. Research shows that people feel the pain of a loss about twice as acutely as they feel the joy of a gain. The concern about a possible *bear market* is a classic *prospect theory* scenario, because it involves tradeoffs. More tangibly, the study concerns itself with decision-making considering inherent uncertainty. The risk/reward tradeoff is the most fundamental tradeoff in finance. Despite this, many advisers were "risk on" in their advice leading up to and at the start of the Covid-19–induced recession. "Induced" is a key word. One way or another, it almost certainly would have happened, anyway. Perhaps more importantly, some advisers were even more "risk on" from the middle of 2020 until early 2022, when central banks brought interest rates down to essentially zero and it seemed as though they would support capital market expansion indefinitely.

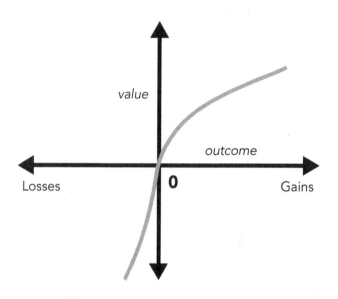

Prospect theory (also known as the *loss-aversion theory*) says investors value gains and losses differently. They place more weight on perceived gains versus perceived losses. Given a choice, investors tend to choose the option presented in terms of potential gains.

An interesting exercise can be conducted based on the feedback loops we all get in the daily news regarding the assumption of market efficiency. In early February 2020, the market was telling us that Covid-19 would have no meaningful impact — that it was "just a virus." By early March 2020, however, it was obvious that a big drop was under way. Then, by the last week of March, the market picked up again. Why? If the news really was that bad, the market should have dropped much more. If everything was fine, markets should not have dropped farther at all. Everyone's personal investing experience was somewhat different, but it seems none fit the efficient-markets model particularly well.

At the time, even the most casual observers would have had to conclude that markets were trading, with particularly violent direction swings from one day to the next, based on something other than just the information that was broadly available and allegedly swiftly reflected in all prices. At the time, new data was almost all negative — so why were there trading sessions when markets went up significantly? The answer is that the market was showing broad confidence in what I call the global Covid playbook. Throughout the Western world, central banks were slashing interest rates to near zero and governments were handing out money to affected citizens. The forward-looking market was speaking. The message: "Don't fight the Fed." It was bold, audacious, and above all, successful. Deliberate, purposeful, coordinated actions designed to restore confidence and optimism had the desired effect. Markets swiftly stabilized and resumed an upward trajectory — but at what cost? Were things genuinely stable again? Remember, many people simply believe what they want to believe. Some engage in *motivated reasoning*, where they simply subscribe to a viewpoint that aligns with their pre-existing biases rather than looking dispassionately at evidence.

The utility function (value) is kinked around the reference point — and for purposes of this discussion, the reference point might be the portfolio's value found on clients' December 31, 2019, statements. For most people, that's the last statement they would have received before Covid-19 hit. It is also a point where, to then, the values of their nest eggs were highest. For many people, the value would have been incrementally higher up to and possibly including February 19, 2020 (the all-time market high to that point), but most people would be unaware of the exact (and incremental) increase. Most people, therefore, would be inclined to "keep score" based on the value of their portfolio as of December 31. Any adviser who understands *prospect theory* should know this and be able to anticipate the likely response of many typical clients, should markets tumble. As fate would have it, markets rebounded too quickly to test the utility function. By the middle of 2020, markets were already moving up comfortably and by the end of Q3, they had regained all that was lost in Q1 of that year. Some advisers pointed to their ability to keep their clients invested as an example of their superior talents of behaviour modification. It was the shortest *bear market* in recorded history. I wonder if they might change their tune if we experience a *bear market* that lasts over a decade.

An interesting and possibly instructive wrinkle from *prospect theory* is that people consistently and predictably take risks to avoid losses yet avoid risks to achieve gains. When markets hit new highs, as in early 2022, there is a compelling case to be made for advisers to focus on profit-taking and capital preservation, considering the perception that the next major move from that point might be downward. Most investors (with and without advice) choose to stay the course, however.

There are other public health lessons, too. Many people believe that stock market contagions are a lot like the contagion of easily transmitted pathogens. In both cases, things can look to be quite normal and certainly no cause for alarm at the outset. Then, it quickly becomes apparent that the problem may well be much, much larger than first suspected.

Research from Robert Shiller is particularly helpful. He has explained how ideas can spread like a virus and that social psychology plays a big role in creating bubbles — and in causing them to burst, too. Shiller has shown that throughout history there has been a tendency for certain dominant ideas to go viral. When thinking about this, it is worth noting that certain ideas come and go in waves, much like how pandemics can have waves of recurrence after the original outbreak.

Optimism gives way to groupthink, which squelches dissenting opinions. Good advisers should make their decisions based on what is best for their clients and should not be overly concerned about what their suppliers, employers, or peers think. Responsible clients need to bear in mind that advisers are human and want to fit in with their pals as much as anyone else.

Maybe the notion of not selling is an ingrained form of thinking fast. It's presumed to be correct. And yet, there must surely be times when selling makes sense. However, since determining when this may be requires thought and analysis, advisers saying "don't sell" might simply be going back to the simple and easy approach: do nothing.

But How Will You Decide?

Decision-making requires clear-minded thinking. Options should be weighed on a balance of probabilities basis where there are a range of possible outcomes (good or bad, very good or very bad, likely or unlikely, etc.).

No one can possibly know for sure what to do in each situation. With that out of the way, it still makes sense to be mindful of possible motives that might not be obvious.

For instance, bank-owned advisory firms are highly concerned about reputational risk and are often more prescriptive in what their advisers say, do, and recommend. When an adviser says they are "independent," probe further. What, exactly, does "independent" mean? Do they read the company's analysts' reports? Do they subscribe to the company's newsletter? Is there a relatively tight recommended list that products and securities must be drawn from? Basically, do they conform to the company's worldview? Note that I'm not saying that worldview is good or bad, necessarily, only that you should probe to see how truly independent your adviser is.

Assuming you have satisfied yourself that your adviser really is independent, you might still want to understand what that looks like. What kind of model will the adviser use in deciding? The answer to that question is the basis for *decision theory*, which has two primary models. A normative model is one that asks what the answer should be (doing what is right), and a process model is one that asks how the problem is solved (doing it the "right way"). Normative models aim to answer the question "If you are trying to solve a problem, what would the best solution look like?" For portfolio management, how does one do a professional and responsible job in seeking suitable returns while simultaneously managing the associated risk? Process models aim to answer the question: "What's the best way to solve this problem?"

Stated differently, *decision theory* can be broken into two branches: normative *decision theory*, which analyzes the outcomes of decisions or determines the optimal decisions given constraints and assumptions; and descriptive *decision theory*, which analyzes how people make their decisions. Outcome versus process.

The theory is concerned with making the best decisions in an uncertain world where no one knows what's in store. The analysis is aimed at finding tools, methodologies, and software to help people make better decisions. How might the typical adviser make a recommendation or decision? And what if the assumptions that lead to the decisions are wrong?

PART II

Good decision-making criteria should lead to better decisions. People who for whatever reason feel good about their outcomes seldom take the time to reflect on the process that led to their decision. That can lead to *attribution bias*.

Rosemary Stewart is a British professor of organizational behaviour. She encourages decision-makers to discern between their circle of concern and their circle of influence. There are many things that might concern you, but can you really influence outcomes based on your decisions? The thought exercise requires not only that the decision-maker can accurately distinguish between the two, but also that they can make a clear-eyed assessment of just how much of an impact they can really have.

How do financial advisers define their roles? Advisers have varying amounts of discretion regarding how to spend their time or focus their attention. Two people with the same title and at the same firm could do very different things, depending on how they operationally define their jobs — considering demands, constraints, and choices, and their values and beliefs about how capital markets function. How does your adviser define their job? What does that job consist of? Does your adviser honestly know what is and is not possible?

Possible answers might include stock, fund, or ETF picking (or any combination of them), financial planning, strategic asset allocation, tactical asset allocation, sector rotation, comprehensive wealth management, intergenerational wealth transfer, and constructive behaviour modification. None of these answers is right or wrong, necessarily, but they will clearly reflect your adviser's worldview. There are a wide number of things that might be of concern to an adviser, but the focus should be squarely on those things that can be influenced. You might be interested in what the central bank does on Tuesday, but no amount of interest from you is going to change the bank's decision.

Financial advisers need to recognize that they can allocate time and attention, which are scarce. They can take risks, or not. They can ask for discretion, or not. They can lead, or follow. They can be reactive, or proactive. So that we're clear on where the circles differ, here's a quick summary:

Circle of Concern

o   Monetary policy
o   Fiscal policy
o   Stock market moves
o   Shape of the yield curve

Circle of Influence

o   Strategic asset allocation
o   Risk-profile matching, meaningful discovery (including risk tolerance)
o   Investment selection
o   Tax loss selling; superficial loss avoidance
o   Financial planning (do it, but use reasonable assumptions)
o   Individual buy/sell decisions

The last bullet is telling. If an adviser is spending most of their time and energy picking stocks or the like, they are almost certainly wasting their time. Research shows that security selection explains little regarding overall performance. If you're spending most of your time working on a problem that makes very little difference, that's a clear indication that your time might be better spent elsewhere. No one is disputing the fact that individuals have influence over the buy and sell decisions, it's just that those decisions have very little utility.

Parsing Fact from Fiction

One of the phrases that has become commonplace in the modern lexicon is *fake news*, a term that some people use to discredit real, fact-based news. The irony, of course, is that the same people who allege that their opponents are quoting *fake news* are themselves engaging in precisely that activity, by telling opposing narratives (sometimes called *alternative facts*) that are put forward as being legitimate. In politics and in life, it seems many people have difficulty determining which of these competing narratives is correct.

The next two chapters deal with case studies on *motivated reasoning* and narrative fallacies as applied to decision-making in capital markets and personal finance. The challenge for everyone is to separate the dispassionate truth from the narratives that have just enough truth to be plausible.

According to Wikipedia, propaganda is "communication that is used primarily to influence an audience and further an agenda, which may not be objective and may be presenting facts selectively to encourage a particular synthesis or perception or using loaded language to produce an emotional rather than a rational response to the information that is presented."

All manner of groups and associations can and do produce propaganda. There's a small army of strategists, executives, economists, and the like that are essentially propagandists for the financial services industry. They are toying with and manipulating your beliefs and perceptions.

Bullshift is a systemic, pervasive mindset that dominates financial services. It is not unambiguously sinister. It is subtle. It involves many people working with the same optimistic and presumptive framework for causation and decision-making. We need to ask a few questions to set the stage:

o Is an adviser's primary role to keep people calm and invested at all costs, or to offer actionable options based on a realistic analysis of circumstances and events as they unfold?
o If the former, do the ends justify the means?
o If the latter, are the specific elements of advice based on emotion, reason, or both?
o Either way, is it at least possible that the advice to "stay calm and stay invested" is a sort of smoke screen to modify behaviour?
o Is the advice to "stay calm and carry on" just a cover to get people to stay invested?

If one were to channel Niccolò Machiavelli, the argument would be that any ultimate end should be achieved by using the means that reflect an obligation to always do what is best for the client. If you consistently do what is best for the client, the means are justified.

Managing emotions and managing behaviour are sometimes different things. Staying calm and staying invested are not even related, necessarily. The words "stay calm and sell out your positions" don't have the same ring to them, but there's no reason why something like that can't be said. The financial services industry's unwritten "how to think" textbook has, over many years and many market cycles, come to equate selling with emotional panic — as if calm, purposeful selling was somehow impossible.

Predictably, advisers often do as they were taught and offer advice based on how they were conditioned. This might make it seem that advisers just follow their chief economist's recommendations. Culpability is transferred. If a chief strategist at a national firm tells everyone who will listen that they're optimistic that there will be a bounce-back before the end of the year, who's to say they're wrong? Everyone is entitled to an opinion.

One can't reasonably say things are under control and then, when it soon becomes apparent that that's untrue, fall back on the "I didn't know" excuse. If you don't know, you should say you don't know. Acting calm and controlled as though outcomes are certain and then claiming ignorance after the fact when things don't go as planned is just an admission of being in over your head. *Motivated reasoning* is everywhere.

Doing something that has worked in the past does not necessarily mean that the same thing will have even a similar impact this time around. The policy responses employed from 2020 to 2021 were indeed unprecedented in size and scope. No one doubts that. What was very much in doubt at the time was whether those steps would still work once things reverted to being normal. Saying something like "substantial and unprecedented steps have been taken" is comforting for those who are action-oriented and to those who want to project the *illusion of control.* When you try something that has never been tried before, you can't be particularly sure about how it is going to play out. No one knows. How can anyone ever be sure that those unprecedented steps would have a positive impact? Simply saying they have been taken and then presuming they will work out is not enough.

By the beginning of 2022, however, there was a new problem. It had become clear that, although a major public health and economic welfare crisis had been averted, a new problem was emerging to take its place. Inflation was beginning to look uncontrollable in those countries that employed the Covid playbook. Central banks would have to either raise rates and risk destroying the recovery or leave rates at generational lows and risk inflation at generational highs. There is no easy answer to this dilemma. The financial services industry had a hard time devising a plausible narrative to assuage concerns once there was no longer any way to optimistically explain away the problem.

Chapter 7

Case Study on the Coronavirus

How to respond to a world racked by Covid?
Say all that you can to prevent going no bid!

Optimists Aren't Survivors …

THE *BEAR MARKET* OF 2020 was one of the steepest *bear markets* in history, and it was absolutely the shortest. That's better for investor experience, but far worse for investor expectations going forward. When it ended, many advisers congratulated themselves on how well they had coached their clients through a difficult period. The false sense of confidence that almost certainly came out of the experience should give everyone pause. There is simply no polite way to say it: no investor alive today ever had to demonstrate their resolve in taking a truly long-term perspective. Every single drawdown in our lifetimes has been medium-term at most. Some of them, like what happened in 2020, were decidedly short-term.

Optimists tend to overestimate the likelihood of positive events and underestimate potentially negative ones. It is believed that 80 percent of the global population suffers from *optimism bias* to some degree. As some financial advisers are almost insufferably optimistic, the percentages are likely even higher for that group. An overabundance of optimism can lead to unwittingly low-balling the likelihood of encountering potential hazards. Interestingly, about 10 percent of the world's population is thought to have *pessimism bias* — lawyers are often in this group.

This brings us to the crux of the problem. Throughout the careers of essentially every investor and adviser you've ever met, markets have gone mostly up. Even when they dropped, those drops have been relatively modest and short-lived. No one knows for sure how investors would react if they were to encounter a deep and prolonged *bear market*, because no one alive today has had to endure anything of the sort. It's an open question. No one knows for sure because there have been no test cases in our lifetimes. All we know for sure is that financial advisers tend to be overwhelmingly optimistic.

Optimists, it seems, simply don't know what to do when the going gets tough. Darwin wrote of the survival of the fittest. It turns out that sometimes survival depends largely on being able to suppress innate optimism. This brings us to the *Stockdale Paradox*. Medal of Honor recipient Commander James Stockdale realized something ironic when he got home after spending years in captivity during the Vietnam war. Thousands of American servicemen were captured by the North Vietnamese and taken as prisoners. The soldiers were tortured, starved, and interrogated relentlessly. By the time the war ended, only 591 men returned home.

When Stockdale was asked why so many of his men didn't make it, he said identifying the key variable leading to their collective demise was easy: "It was the optimists." It turns out that having a lower set of expectations about the future helps you cope. In short, hope is good, but false hope can be fatal. For POWs, instead of being optimistic, it would have been better to be simply realistic. The lesson is counterintuitive, but instructive.

False hope, the kind that presupposes that everything will be fine if you can just hold on for another few months, can sap your will to soldier on. It turns out that people need to confront their reality as quickly and honestly as possible to make it through. Dante's *Inferno* offers a simple touchstone for those entering the gates of Hell. It bears an inscription that ends with the phrase *"Lasciate ogne speranza, voi ch'intrate,"* which is roughly translated as "Abandon all hope, ye who enter here."

... Neither Are Underperforming Mutual Funds

With actively managed mutual funds, false hope can easily give way to false belief due to *survivorship bias*. That's a form of logical error: people focus on things that made it past the selection process while overlooking those things that did not. It is the all-too-human tendency to view the performance of existing products in the market as a representative sample.

Survivorship bias can lead to overly optimistic beliefs and is particularly problematic when considering the historical performance of actively managed mutual funds. By looking exclusively at the surviving "winners" from the universe of products available at a given point in time, the large number of "losers" that have since been closed is often overlooked. The result is the mistaken impression that the overall performance of the participants was better than it actually was.

For example, if one hundred people enter a marathon and the average time of the finishers is four hours, that creates the impression that the time of the average participant was respectable. If you later learn that sixty of the original one hundred racers failed to finish, you might be left with a different impression. With funds, this happens both because the performance is embarrassing to the company sponsor and because the poor performer fails to gather assets to manage. It has been widely reported that over half the mutual funds created fail to celebrate a tenth anniversary. The drag on overall performance for the average fund investor is widely seen as being substantial.

Despite the information about survivorship being readily available, a large number of advisers continue to recommend actively managed funds to their clients while failing to mention the problem. There's a consensus that this is an example of advisers' collective *motivated reasoning*, not to mention *herding* and *confirmation bias*. Given how widespread the problem is and how thoroughly it has been documented over the past few decades, it is highly unlikely that advisers could credibly claim to be ignorant of the evidence. Despite the evidence, they continue to actively recommend such funds, perhaps because of the comfort that comes with using the only product and business model that many advisers and investors have ever known — which is a form of *status quo bias*.

If the battle-hardened advisers who play the role of behavioural coaches are themselves prone to throwing in the towel while simultaneously ignoring the evidence that some of their product suppliers have done the same, it invites questions about how effective they will be in getting their clients to stay the course in tough times.

. . .

It has been said that financial advisers are "money coaches," who offer context and perspective to assist clients to get through whatever comes. This narrative is built mostly on the assumption that most clients lack those attributes. Of course, the perspective that advisers generally espouse is that things will get better soon enough. It turns out, though, that a positive outlook, while helpful in most instances, is decidedly unhelpful when things turn out to be worse than anticipated. That's when people really need to hunker down. What ordeals do people need to endure in a roaring *bear market*? It's hard to say, until they encounter one.

If things go horribly wrong and markets drop a lot and stay low for a prolonged period, advisers and investors alike will need to focus their energy on survival. Can they? What if the world throws something at them that neither group has ever experienced before? They'd both go through the same ordeal together at the same time and for the first time. Sure, there are textbooks and history books explaining how they might respond, but those reference guides can seem to have little to do with lived experience. When your life's savings are evaporating, the sickness of watching a life's work disappear will almost certainly cause even the most stoic and disciplined investors to lose their cool.

Old warnings and fears will almost certainly resurface. You know the ones. It has been said that the four most dangerous words in investing are

"This time it's different." Everyone puts on a brave face and insists they are a "long-term investor" — at first. But as time wears on and both advisers and investors experience something neither ever experienced before, what stops them from thinking this time really *is* different? What if they simply can't cope? How many will accept that their worst nightmares are coming true and nonetheless resolve to stay the course?

In the past century, there has been one truly awful *bear market*, one far worse than any other — the Great Depression of the 1930s. The problem is that no one investing today has ever had to experience what it was like to live through anything close to a severe and prolonged downturn like that. All the other major *bear markets*, the 1974–1975 crash, caused by oil price shocks, the downturn at the turn of the millennium after the popping of the "dot.com" bubble, and the Global Financial Crisis of 2008–2009, were drawdowns of about 50 percent, and after those, the market regained its value within a couple of years. Modest when compared to the Depression.

There are two important considerations when thinking about how one might react to a major pullback, especially before the depth and length of the drop is known:

o   How much will investments drop in value?
o   How long will it take for those investments to climb back
    to previous levels?

It's the second that is the most crucial. Financial advisers constantly tell their clients to "take a long-term view," but there is no real consensus on how long that is. Five years? Ten years? Twenty years? The rest of your life? People grow accustomed to outcomes when they seem consistent and predictable. Stocks rebounding relatively quickly after they drop sharply is a situation experienced relatively frequently. It has been comforting for investors. Every single time a North American investor has experienced a drop in the value of their portfolio, that investor has also experienced a swift recovery. Why should the next time be any different? But what if the horror doesn't end until the end of the decade?

Let's make a simple comparison to get a sense of what we're dealing with. Think of running. Body types for the runners differ considerably based on the length of the race. Those who run the hundred metres look muscular. Those who run marathons look waifish. Remarkable speeds require the ability to produce raw, short bursts of power and can only be sustained over extremely short distances. Anyone running a gruelling 42.2-kilometre race needs to get rid of every gram of excess weight to maximize endurance. Look at the following race lengths:

o   100 metres
o   800 metres
o   1.5 kilometres
o   5 kilometres
o   10 kilometres
o   21.1 kilometres (half marathon)
o   42.2 kilometres (marathon)

Think about the different body types of runners and how they change as races lengthen. Those who run only the hundred metres are called "sprinters." Depending on whom you talk to, sprinters might be those running as far as eight hundred metres. Those running in 1.5-kilometre and five-kilometre races are called "middle-distance runners." Finally, those running ten kilometres or more are "long-distance runners."

Now, think of investing and pretend a kilometre is a year. In this environment, 1.5 kilometres (also called a "metric mile") is the equivalent of about eighteen months — middle distance. Only those with a time horizon of ten years or more could be the investing equivalents of long-distance runners. One last detail to complete the metaphor. Where runners have body types, investors have attitudes. To be successful, investors and advisers need an attitude that equates to a person with the body type who runs ten kilometres. That is what the minimum definition of long-term looks like. Other than Japanese investors, no one today has ever experienced a six- or seven-year downturn without getting back to where they started. Basically, no investor today ever ran the equivalent of a ten-kilometre race, yet they all insist they are prepared and able to run at least a half-marathon if necessary.

In addition to *optimism bias* and *overconfidence* clouding judgment when there is the chance that a prolonged downturn will occur, there is also the real threat of *recency bias* creeping into decision-making. In the five weeks from mid-February to late March in 2020, stocks throughout most of the Western world dropped by about 33 percent. It was one of the steepest declines in history. People were petrified. Then, as a direct result of unprecedented fiscal stimulus and changes to monetary policy all around the world, the steep market decline was not only stopped, but quickly reversed. Never had central banks around the world put up such a monumental and courageous fight. It worked, and that's the problem. Had banks not intervened, the public health measures taken to battle the spread of Covid-19 would almost certainly have plunged the world into a massive recession — and possibly a depression. Investors and advisers became complacent because what might have otherwise been a catastrophe was averted. Both acted as though they had won a long-distance race that, in fact, had been more like an eight-hundred-metre sprint.

Precisely because the sudden drop was short-lived and recent, the perception set in that central bankers and governments around the world had "solved the puzzle of the market cycle" and "had the backs of investors" in a way that made investing all but foolproof. Basically, people felt they could be reckless because policies allowing for reckless behaviour were being rewarded. That's called hubris and it is very dangerous.

Everyone says they are taking a long-term view to investing until a long, protracted, painful-like-nothing-they've-ever-experienced-before *bear market* steps up and bites them. Then their plans change. The two rules about panic selling are these:

> **Rule 1:** Don't panic.
>
> **Rule 2:** If, for some reason, you choose to ignore rule 1, be among the first to do so.

Humans are predictably irrational. Most investors follow a consistent and predictable pattern of behaviour when markets drop. What is so disconcerting about *optimism bias* may be that it can lead to an inadequate assessment of potential hazards.

Most of us would likely self-identify as adherents to rule 1 if a market begins to drop. We will almost certainly stay that way if markets drop by 10 percent, 20 percent, or 30 percent or for one quarter, two quarters, or three quarters. Garden-variety market drops are not the concern. The concern is how people might react to what could go down as the biggest, deepest, longest downturn of their lives. What if the drop was more than 60 percent and markets were nowhere close to returning to their previous levels five years after the drop started?

Thinking positively facilitates envisioning what is possible. By allowing us to be courageous and innovative, optimism allows us to take chances we might not otherwise take and to succeed where we might not try otherwise. The level of *optimism bias* varies according to our mental state and current circumstances, and there are ways to temper or increase it.

Even though this is the case, how many people attempt to do so? Understanding where you sit on the optimism spectrum can help you adjust for your bias — and maybe even make better choices.

At the root of the problem are two optimistic assumptions: first, that we possess more positive traits than the average person; second, that we have some control over the world around us. Neither is necessarily true. We fool ourselves to feel better.

Let's focus on what it means to be an optimistic investor in a raging *bear market*. The feeling is like having your spouse leave you, having your favourite pet die, and being told you have cancer — all in the same week. People claim to be resilient. They say they're cautiously optimistic, which means they tend to hope for the best, but they never really prepare themselves for what might lie ahead. Out of curiosity, have you ever met anyone who is "recklessly pessimistic" or even "dispassionately realistic"? There's simply no corresponding antonym in our lexicon, yet this kind of self-assessment is pervasive.

With marathons, even experienced runners can "hit the wall," where for some reason they simply cannot go on. They stop. They are often in physical pain. Sometimes, they even question how they got themselves into this situation. Many pick themselves up and soldier on, but the people who hit the wall are often forced to give up on the goal they set out for themselves when they embarked on their journey. So it is with investing. At some point, the dream of a comfortable retirement at age sixty-five or whatever is abandoned when those rose-coloured assumptions no longer seem possible.

Take a moment to think of how you would react to this situation. Stop and reflect on how it would feel in the pit of your stomach as you head to work in the morning. How would it feel when you come home to your loved ones? How would you sleep? What would you even look forward to?

Now, think of financial advisers. Victor Frankl once said that having a purpose in life can make all the difference when you're trying to keep going in the face of adversity. Having meaning in your life provides the strength to keep going, no matter what. For advisers, their meaning — in fact, their identity in many cases — is derived from their ability to help people reach their financial goals. A major drawdown would be an assault on the typical adviser's purpose in life!

Advisers' accounts will be down, too, of course, but because their clients' accounts will be way down, advisers' revenues will be much lower as well. It's one thing to lose (say) half the value of your investable assets if you're an investor. But imagine losing half your assets, having your take-home pay cut in half, and still going to work — day after day after day. Dealing with miserable clients and coaching them to continue to hang on could become a daunting chore.

Advisers have sunny dispositions because that frame of mind helps them help their clients cope with the mundane, annoying, and tiresome obstacles we all face in the journey of getting what we want out of life. Will those sunny dispositions serve them well if their clients' obstacles seem more like life-altering challenges? The industry-wide optimism suggests the best advisers would encourage clients to buy more stocks after the value of their investments has dropped, because rebalancing is proper and prudent. That's the theory. In practice, we all know that plenty of clients will call Bullshift and will simply refuse to comply. We all know that plenty of investors will sell. It has happened all too often in garden-variety *bear markets*.

As a person who knows many advisers personally, I can assure you that they are genuinely happy when clients succeed. In fact, advisers feel a good deal of satisfaction when clients succeed — in part because they feel they had a hand in that success. Imagine how gut-wrenching it would be if those same bright-eyed, cheery advisers lost their will to carry on. After all, advisers are human, too. When the behavioural coaches lose their will, they too might capitulate. That, in turn, would almost certainly cause markets to fall even further — to levels that would have previously seemed impossible. This needs to be repeated: other than Japan, in the past 30-plus years there are no precedents in the modern Western world to help us anticipate what might happen to human behaviour in a depression.

When the one who is supposed to encourage you to keep a stiff upper lip is being barraged with phone calls and emails from desperate clients terrified by what they see and read, it's only natural that your adviser will become shellshocked. Here's where retail investors need to be vigilant.

The two rules of panic selling will apply. From the beginning, advisers will insist that the only rule is rule 1. Clients will continue to hound them and express their pain. Naturally, advisers will want to take away that pain. Some of them will give up. They will succumb. They will allow their clients to apply rule 2, except many of them will have resisted rule 2 as a matter of pride, identity, and industry-wide behavioural mantras. For those people — advisers and investors alike — it'll be worse. Rule 2 says if you're going to sell, do so early.

When markets go down and stay down, there's no telling when resolve will be broken. In many instances, it will not be early. For some, their mis-calibration of their own ability to hang on will bring tragic results. Some will hang on longer than ever before, yet will learn that "longer than ever before" might still not be "long enough." This applies equally to advisers and investors.

The message is simple: for most people most of the time, *optimism bias* and Bullshift work quite well. That has clearly been the case until now. The thing to remember is that if the mindset fails, it could fail spectacularly. Apart from a brief downturn, the markets experienced no immediate sig-nificant damage as a result of the Covid-19 crisis; there was no prolonged downturn. That sort of thing was for people's great-grandparents. People came to think of such devastating downturns as ancient history. It wasn't supposed to happen to them, and as a result, they simply will not be pre-pared if it does happen to them.

One of the old adages people like to cite when talking about portfolios and their associated risk profiles is that "the best portfolio is the one you can stick to." The problem, of course, is that most people cannot accurately predict what they can and cannot stick to before they face the raw emotional pain in the moment. To wit: if you don't really know what you can stick to, how can you possibly know what the best portfolio is? For most people, fear and greed are more powerful motivators than a commitment to a long-term outlook.

Central Banker Bullshift

When the coronavirus struck, stock market valuations were high, and some commentators were already calling for a recession due to the U.S. yield curve having inverted nine months earlier. Even before anyone ever heard of Covid-19, many felt a recession was possible or probable. The pandemic merely hastened what these people felt was inevitable when markets tumbled in early 2020.

Then, like fairy-tale heroes, central bankers came riding to the rescue. It's important to note that the global monetary policy playbook was remarkably well coordinated. In Canada, the U.S., the European Union, and throughout the industrialized world, rates were swiftly slashed to essentially zero, and in record time. Markets started dropping in February 2020, and by March, every major central bank had engaged in a massive stimulus effort, the likes of which had never been seen before.

Central bankers insisted they had "learned some valuable lessons" from the Global Financial Crisis (GFC) of 2007–2009. What they did then was essentially correct, but quantitatively modest — or so they said. But they promised to lower rates soon and keep them low longer, so a full recovery could ensue. Governments of all political stripes throughout the Western world seized the opportunity to spend like never before, providing fiscal stimulus to capitalize on the monetary backstop. It didn't matter what your political stripe was prior to the pandemic, there were no fiscal conservatives to be found anywhere in government in the midst of it. Even opposition parties signed on to the notion of spending like there was no tomorrow. The cost to the public coffers was negligible as long as rates were effectively zero.

A little over a year into the great stimulus experiment, signs of inflation began to emerge. This has happened various times in the past, most notably in Weimar Germany after the First World War. Some pundits expressed alarm that central bankers were deviating from their core mandate of price stability. Others insisted we should all remain calm and central bankers knew what they were doing. The view was that since inflation had remained in check globally for about thirty years, any uptick would be short-lived. Who could doubt their credibility?

Around May of 2021, central banks began to change their messaging. Rather than fight inflation, they would let it "run hot" to allow the delicate economic recovery to gain a stronger footing. Instead of aiming for relatively modest inflation of 2 percent, bankers said they would relax their core mandate so the recovery could take hold. The last thing they wanted to do was to kill off economic growth, having averted disaster one year earlier. They insisted there was nothing to worry about as slightly higher inflation would be "transitory." Better safe than sorry. The media offered mixed commentary, but generally gave the bankers the benefit of the doubt.

Throughout the second half of 2021, stock markets and inflation rates continued to rise while central bankers watched but did nothing. They insisted no action was needed, they said they were were monitoring the situation carefully, and they assured all concerned that they would act firmly and swiftly if inflation got out of control. But the warning signs increased. Month after month in country after country, inflation was on the rise. Central bankers continued with their reassurances, and many economic and political commentators provided the intellectual cover needed, insisting that central bankers knew best. After all, a thirty-year global track record of controlled inflation buys a lot of goodwill.

Of course, central bankers and media outlets are subject to Bullshift, too. In a world where investment psychology and confidence are half the battle, there is a lot to be gained by keeping a smile on everyone's face.

The skeptics were outnumbered, mostly because *motivated reasoning* was taking hold. People simply wanted the central bankers to be right. As such, there was not enough consideration given to the idea that the stimulus provided might be overkill and might cause a prolonged bout of inflation. Even if that did not come to pass, there would likely be a time once the stimulus had subsided, and the situation had normalized, that economic growth would stall.

In retrospect, it now seems that a better policy response would have been to begin raising rates, perhaps by twenty-five basis points (0.25 percent) per central bank meeting, around mid-2021. It needs to be stressed that no one knows for sure if this would have made a difference, but by early 2022 there was little doubt central bankers around the world had goofed. We had been going too fast for too long. Alas, hindsight is always 20/20. There is simply no way of knowing if it would have been better to begin the process of normalization sooner.

With the concern that stocks, bonds, and real estate were all in bubble territory as a direct result of the coordinated stimulus, there was trepidation in some circles about the strength of the market; but there was overconfidence bordering on denial in others. Major asset classes needed a large metaphorical dose of medication to overcome what was obviously overstimulation, but no one would prescribe it. Instead, all assets got hyperactive and everyone got giddy.

Just because the central bank–manufactured asset bubbles hadn't popped yet did not mean we were not dealing with bubbles or that they wouldn't pop. One reason the party persisted was that investors wanted to believe it would go on indefinitely. Assurances that central bankers would not raise rates allowed some investors to morph into speculators.

By the beginning of 2022, however, the inflationary trends were undeniable, and it was obvious the timing for normalization had to be drastically accelerated. Forward guidance on the timing, size, and number of hikes had to be communicated in no uncertain terms. The game had changed, and it was time for central bankers to admit their collective misreading of the environment. Specifically, supply-chain disruptions caused by the lingering effects of the pandemic, coupled with a major war in Europe, meant prices were going to stay high for finance, fuel, and food.

The jig was finally up. Central bankers were losing credibility every month with new inflation data released. It became painfully obvious that what we were experiencing was not transitory, and not even cresting. Severe, activist intervention was needed immediately.

Central banks always act swiftly when they get to play the role of hero. They are less swift when called upon to play the villain. In theory, central bankers are neither heroes nor villains but regulators of inflation rates and steady-handed guarantors of price stability. They were swift in 2020 because everyone wanted them to be swift but slothful until 2022 because, notwithstanding comments made by some purists, everyone wanted them to be slothful.

The new challenge was to engineer a so-called soft landing in an inflationary environment. But things had changed. Compared to when the pandemic began, household debt was far higher, government debt was far higher, inflation was far higher, and interest rates were still near all-time lows. It was an unenviable challenge, but monetary policy makers found themselves in a bed they themselves had made.

The consensus viewpoint was that major hikes and purposeful action would have a predictable response. It would effectively manufacture a recession. By rights, the world should have entered a recession in early 2020, but central bankers delayed that recession and likely made it more severe by being swift when it was easy to act and slow when it was hard. The Bullshift we see in the financial services industry was promulgated by central bankers, just as it is by optimistic advisers and a media complex that wants to keep the good times rolling.

On May 20, 2022, the S&P 500 had officially fallen into bear territory (a peak-to-trough decline of 20 percent or more). Owing to the butchering of bonds we were experiencing, an American 50/50 portfolio (half stocks, half bonds) was down by 13.4 percent by that date. Canadian central bankers were the most responsible (i.e., the least irresponsible) because their rates were the highest within the sample, while inflation was lowest, and Canada was the first major jurisdiction to begin raising rates. Real central bank rates (overnight central bank rate minus inflation) were as follows:

Canada	-5.8% (1% rate, 6.8% inflation)
U.S.	-7.4% (0.875% rate, 8.3% inflation)
Eurozone	-7.9% (-.5% rate, 7.4% inflation)
U.K.	-8% (1% rate, 9.0% inflation)

Central bankers found themselves way behind the curve and in desperate need of playing catch-up. Inflation was at a thirty-year high and climbing steadily, yet they seemed content to do nothing until the situation became desperate.

By the summer of 2022, the broad-based perpetual bullishness that investors had come to know for the past several decades came face to face with the larger economic imperative of keeping inflation in check, no matter what the consequences might be. From the spring of 2020 until the end of 2021, central bankers were universally accommodative and, as a result, people thought they were being prudent by being bullish. *Recency bias* was playing games with people's psyches and the collective behaviour of retail investors failed to adjust to the newfound hawkishness of central bankers. Thinking the recent past would be a reliable guide to the foreseeable future, most people chose to stay invested even though markets were dropping and further rate hikes were clearly on the horizon.

So, what have we learned? First, everyone seemed determined to fight the last war. Given that the response to the GFC was too timid, policymakers erred on the side of stronger intervention in 2020. In hindsight, many now think the Covid-19 response would have been best for the GFC and the GFC response best for Covid-19. Both were correct in direction and both more or less worked, but the appropriate interventions for each seem to have been switched. Even the right policies, if not timed or calibrated properly, can bring a whole new set of problems that policy experts call "unintended consequences."

The lesson in all this is that central bankers are human, and micro-managing the disparate elements of a modern economy is not for the faint of heart. Many people were pleasantly shocked at how swift and purposeful a central bank (and national government) response to a pandemic can be. The speed and magnitude of the intervention were unprecedented in every way. That response, in turn, led to a massive run-up in asset prices for virtually all asset classes. It also exacerbated several challenging socio-economic conditions that had been lingering just below the surface. There is little doubt that the easy money policies of central bankers not only gave rise to inflation, but also fuelled populism, as well as social and income inequality. Markets boomed because central bankers provided an environment that allowed them to boom. A degree of *cognitive dissonance* took hold and no one wanted the party to end, so central bankers were late in taking away the punch bowl. But even great parties must end eventually.

What This Means Going Forward

Research shows that financial advisers are almost universally optimistic in their outlook toward markets in general. Most can legitimately stick to a risky portfolio in ordinary downturns. A problem might occur when advisers and investors experience something severe. Advisers might be able to handle a 30 percent decline in their portfolio and their clients may have said they could handle something similar. But what if the adviser unwittingly projected a bit too much optimism to the client and simply believed it was reasonable to proceed accordingly?

The risk to investors is that well-intended advisers might make an assessment error just like the central bankers did. The adviser might say, "I wouldn't put you into a portfolio that I couldn't handle personally," but that presumes the client's risk tolerance and risk capacity is like the adviser's. Even if intentions are good and the adviser believes they can keep the client invested through thick and thin, what if the client loses their cool? That could be described as the adviser being overconfident in their ability to assess client risk, or overconfident in thinking that they can manage negative reactions and modify client behaviours accordingly.

Many advisers have likely been at least somewhat socialized by their industry's norms and attitudes. That's not necessarily bad, but we need to recognize that when the advice is impervious to circumstances, advisers may be unintentionally putting their clients in danger.

Many advisers are unwittingly focused on the wrong things. Most of the time, they should likely just build cheap, diversified portfolios that are in line with their clients' risk profiles. Investors need to insist that advisers maintain a focus on their circle of influence and, in the process, assist them by refusing to discuss, beyond a superficial level, things that are merely in their circle of concern.

No one can reliably pick stocks or time markets, so the point above needs to be taken seriously. That said, just because it cannot be done reliably does not necessarily mean it should not be attempted. Just know that the odds are against you. No one had flown before the Wright brothers. Does that mean they should not have attempted to fly? The concern for focus and discipline is real. Some advisers think they need to stay focused on getting their clients to show discipline by not selling. Ever. Surely to goodness, there must be some instances where selling is warranted, prudent, practical, clear-headed, non-reactive, and purposeful.

To hear many commentators tell it, the *flight to quality* (e.g., from growth stocks to value stocks) is always sensible and prudent in a *bear market*. It might be okay in a modest correction (less than 20 percent drop), but what about in a raging bear (more than 40 percent drop)? How is going to cash, which neither appreciates nor depreciates in the short term, inappropriate when going to *high quality stocks* (that "only" drop by half as much as the market as a whole) is considered appropriate?

You always have an option. Richard Thaler's choice architecture shows that the choices we make can be influenced by how the options are framed and presented. Other studies have also shown that the way options are presented can have a major impact on which are chosen. What's worse — acting as though there are no alternatives, or being oblivious to framing impacts regarding the alternatives in front of you?

Alas, some advisers act as though selling anything at any time is "not an option." It categorically is. Selling might not always work out. It might not always be the "correct choice" with the benefit of hindsight, but it is always an option. Such advisers literally don't even think about selling ... and they expend most of their energy trying to disabuse their clients of the desire to do so.

The Prisoner's Dilemma

There are applications from *game theory* that are applicable to the behaviour of capital markets. For instance, a *prisoner's dilemma* is a situation where individual decision-makers have an incentive to choose an option that creates a less than ideal outcome for those same individuals' group. It can reward selfishness at the expense of team play ... greed is good ... every man for himself. Most *game theory* concepts involve choices between the competing interests of rival individuals or rival companies; but what if the concept is moved from a micro level (a scenario with only two or three individual players) to a macro level (a scenario with many players)? The same basic principles would apply, but the consequences would be spread out over many, many smaller decisions.

The classic scenario that gives this concept its name involves two suspects that are captured, then separated and interrogated individually. The law enforcement people have only modest evidence against either of the alleged perpetrators, but if they interrogate them separately, they can offer each a plea-bargained deal (e.g., a reduced sentence) for ratting out their accomplice. If one rats out the other, they might indeed get less jail time, provided the accomplice remains silent. However, if each rats, then there would be enough strong evidence to convict both — and with a maximum sentence to boot. Alternatively, if both remain silent, the evidence might not be enough to gain a conviction at all. The dilemma for the suspect is one of anticipating what their partner in crime is likely to do under duress. Remaining silent is best if everyone co-operates, but there's also a strong personal incentive for each perpetrator to rat, to improve their own chance for freedom.

In capital markets, the roles are somewhat analogous. When it comes to the group psychology of investor decision-making in a context of uncertainty, financial advisers play the role of law enforcement officials and investors play the prisoners. The dilemma involves trying to predict whether markets will go up or down — and then deciding how to behave. Obviously, no one knows for sure how markets will move, but to some extent, mass psychology (*herding*) can have an impact on how things play out. As with the decision about whether to co-operate with authorities when accused of a crime, investors need to decide whether they are going to sell when markets start dropping. In both instances, it would help considerably if there were some sort of reliable knowledge about what their counterparts were intending. People would know what to do if they had a reliable idea of what other people were likely to do.

In finance, this is especially true when it seems at least somewhat likely that there is a *bear market* on the horizon. Since *bear markets* come around about once a decade, the approach taken involves human interactions that are repeated with at least a little regularity. A classic *prisoner's dilemma* is typically played only once. If played repeatedly, it is an *iterated prisoner's dilemma*. Therefore, investor behaviour in protracted *bear markets* is more of an iterated *prisoner's dilemma*, where the players can choose strategies that reward co-operation or punish defection in multiple iterations and over a long timeframe. The players (individual investors) repeatedly interact with the same individuals (other investors), so they can learn from experience to better anticipate likely moves in the future and capitalize on them.

This iterative nature can alter the decisions that are made. People do learn from experience. Accordingly, if they've been paying attention to how people reacted in the past, advisers and investors alike should have a reasonably good approximation of what might happen the next time they're in a similar situation.

The ploy is something advisers are intuitively aware of. Instead of acting like the cops trying to get prisoners to confess, they use whatever moral suasion they can muster to keep their clients from selling. Thus, the industry in general and advisers in particular engage in a form of collective action that encourages "co-operative behaviour" (i.e., not selling) through a variety of means in the hope of attaining more collectively beneficial outcomes. Fortuitously, this frequently does work out for the best. Most of the time, getting most clients to hold on to most of their positions while markets experience turbulence is what is best for most investors.

Of course, some people have developed their own behavioural biases and tendencies. In a society that features competing interests, some people may lead groups of individuals to choose alternative outcomes that can be quite sensible. If there's going to be a massive rush to sell, then it is likely best to be among the first to do so, as prices will be dropping consistently throughout the experience.

Group dynamics points to how a variation on the *prisoner's dilemma* could play out in a *bear market*. Instead of law enforcement representatives being better off by getting the participants to change their behaviour, we have financial advisory professionals being worse off if they cannot get people to change their behaviour. Many investors, if left to their own devices, would be more likely to sell — and sooner rather than later — if it weren't for the intervention of their adviser counselling them to hold their positions.

What results is a variation on a similar concept called *the tragedy of the commons*. It may be in everyone's collective advantage to act in a communal way and not sell. Think of what happened to the fisheries on the Grand Banks a generation ago. Before overfishing, everyone understood that countries ought to co-operate to conserve and reinvest in the publicly available natural resource to be able to continue consuming it. Once the technology advanced to the point where fish could be almost literally vacuumed up from the ocean floor, incentives changed, and all fishers quickly took as much as they could before others got there. They also had an immediate incentive to harvest as much of the resource as possible, thereby depleting the resource. Trust, co-operation, and goodwill were required to keep things going. When those attributes failed to persist, the result was catastrophic.

As with the cod stocks, finding a way to get investors to co-operate for the greater good could make everyone better off. In *bear markets*, advisers and investors are collectively playing a game of chicken. As with the military metaphors used during the Covid-19 pandemic (stay safe; we'll get through this; we're all in this together), financial authorities try to encourage desirable group behaviour for what they believe is the greater good.

It seems some advisers are simply not considering *prospect theory* in their recommendations. *Prospect theory* involves the tradeoffs involved with decision-making considering uncertainty. As everyone knows, the risk/reward tradeoff is likely the most fundamental tradeoff in finance. Any adviser who understands *prospect theory* should know this and be able to anticipate the likely response of many typical clients should markets tumble. The perverse lesson is that many of us are more prepared to take risks to avoid losses and more willing to miss out on gains if the tradeoff is to avoid losses. For this reason alone, there ought to be more products available that offer inverse market participation with a limit on what can be lost if markets go rocketing up.

Research done by Robert Shiller is particularly helpful. His book *Irrational Exuberance* explains how ideas can spread like a virus (which is ironic) and that social psychology plays a big role in building up valuation, i.e., in creating bubbles, and in causing them to burst. His 2019 book *Narrative Economics* shows that we often develop narratives after the fact to explain what happened and why. These narratives are often far removed from the evidence. Shiller says his cyclically adjusted price earnings (CAPE) calculations are not useful for the purpose of market timing. The methodology intends to smooth out valuations over a decade and to control for the impact of inflation, because valuations can stay inordinately high for a very long time. Experience has shown that, when taken over longer time horizons, CAPE readings are often extremely accurate in predicting future long-term annualized returns. The higher the CAPE reading, the lower the return over the next decade. By early 2022, the CAPE on the S&P 500 was the second highest it had ever been.

This is another example of how financial management and financial planning would do well to collaborate more closely. There's more about this in the next chapter, but it should be noted that industry-wide planning assumption guidelines are updated annually and based on complex methodology, including a variety of reputable inputs. Some of these are historical, but conspicuously do not refer to Shiller's CAPE work, even though it is highly credible.

Clearly, some advisers suffer from overconfidence. In contrast, there are others that are almost totally unconcerned about what their suppliers, employers, or peers think and do. They think for themselves. As an investor, you need to find ways to distinguish between the two. Ask questions. The former group is not necessarily harmful, but it is potentially harmful — especially if both you and your adviser are oblivious to your adviser's optimistic predisposition.

Daniel Kahneman uses "thinking, fast and slow" as a paradigm. Perhaps the notion of not selling is an ingrained form of "System 1" for some advisers. It is fast, knee-jerk, and presumptive. There must surely be some instances when selling early makes sense. However, since the conscious decision to sell requires careful thought and analysis (including accountability for the decision afterwards), advisers might simply be reverting to the simple, easy, prescriptive (and lazy) approach of going with the flow. They do nothing. Oftentimes, nothing is the right thing to do, too — but not always. What about those instances?

This brings us back to the concept of *normative optimality*. What would a rational, self-aware, self-interested investor do? Of course, we all purport to have those attributes. A normative model is one that asks what the answer to a problem should be, whereas a process model is one that asks how it is solved.

A normatively optimal solution suggests that if you are trying to solve a problem, you should seek out the best way to solve it. As it pertains to portfolio management in a world where valuations are clearly stretched, how does one do a professional and responsible job in seeking returns while simultaneously managing risk?

When considering advisers who were long only — did they at least consider using stop losses? What factor inputs were weighed when making buy/sell and asset allocation recommendations? When was the last time they rebalanced, and did they consider tactically overweighting income investments as part of the exercise? The reluctance to sell and preserve portfolio values could be a huge black mark against embedded-compensation products. If an adviser gets paid a percentage for assets under management (AUM), there's a perfectly good reason to promote loss minimization to preserve revenues.

Once again, no one knows in advance what course of action is best. That's another way of saying that either course could turn out to be appropriate after the fact. Given that either option might be in the client's interest after the fact, why is only one recommended before the fact?

If an adviser's job really is to be a behavioural coach, shouldn't getting clients to sell early be considered a win if that client is likely to lose their nerve and sell later at a lower value? Say a market drops by 20 percent. What should a responsible adviser say? The industry has made a point of noting that to get out and then get back in, people need to be right two times ... and no one can time markets reliably. Of course, no one knows in advance when a market will drop, why it will drop, how long the drop will last, or how deep the drop will be. This is often trotted out as a reason to hold indefinitely and indiscriminately. Indeed, no one knows.

Alternatively, if you don't want to take a behavioural approach, there are parallels in traditional economics, too. Introductory microeconomics assumes that the first objective for a firm is to maximize profits and that if the first objective cannot be realized, the next best thing is to minimize losses. How is this any different? Advisers don't always act in a way that is consistent with *neoclassical economics* when giving advice. Selling when a big drawdown seems probable strikes me as being sensible. Conversely, how can anyone truly know what is "probable" when making forward-looking statements?

The previous question not only defines the crux of the problem, but it also offers the implicit rationale for the ubiquitous prescription. If no one knows and markets usually go up year over year and always go up eventually, why not just hold?

In the culture of advice-giving, if the client sells at any point, the adviser is generally deemed to have failed. Basically, if the adviser defines their role as keeping clients invested come hell or high water, then a sell order is tantamount to failure.

This might be a good opportunity to check in with one of the truly great economists of all time. John Maynard Keynes is a twentieth-century British economist who is among the most influential people ever regarding business cycles, the role of government, and the like. He was keenly aware of behavioural aspects that crop up, but is nonetheless revered as a traditional economist. Among other things, Keynes has also said, "When my information changes, I alter my conclusions."

We are all prone to groupthink, and if everyone does something, that makes it socially acceptable. And so it is with the predictable advice not to sell no matter what is going on in the world outside. Are some advisers more concerned with factual evidence, or social conformity? Keynes's intellectual flexibility was remarkable. Some modern advisers, when faced with emerging evidence that behavioural considerations require greater consideration, often choose to simply continue doing their job the way they always have. Accordingly, investors need to remain vigilant. Some in the advice industry seem to be dangerously wedded to previous attitudes and outlooks, even if credible new information calls those attitudes and outlooks into question.

To be clear, I'm not saying that holding onto one's securities isn't necessarily the best option. I'm simply saying that others may be overstating their predictable advice that it definitively is the best option.

Old habits die hard. A generation ago, the primary investment vehicles were individual securities and embedded-compensation mutual funds. Curiously, some advisers (those who used primarily securities) could make more in commissions by trading. Mutual fund advisers, however, would see their income drop sharply if clients went to cash. Being invested in an embedded-compensation product meant trailing commissions for the adviser of record. If clients' funds were switched from equities to fixed income, embedded compensation to the adviser would be cut in half. If they were switched to money market products, they would be cut to nearly nothing. If the funds were sold outright, the adviser's income would stop altogether.

This format of having advisory compensation tied to the products being recommended — and then having different products compensate advisers differently — created a massive incentive for advisers to keep clients invested in equities. This invites a concern about concepts like principal-agent relationships, the challenges of asymmetrical information, conflicts of interest, and incentives in general. These problems have been explored in great detail previously, so I will not delve into them here.

The spin on this incentive has always been that staying invested is what is best for clients. However, it now seems apparent that the word "always" has some exceptions ... and that what was purportedly a wrinkle that was good for investors might have actually been a baked-in bias in favour of mutual fund manufacturers and distributors at the direct expense of the interests of their "valued investor" clients. What is more meaningful (and more motivational in terms of behaviour change) is that advisers were paid more to keep clients in stock positions that were dropping in value than they were for having them in bond positions that were holding their own or appreciating. The mutual fund industry had baked in a systemic *compensation bias* in favour of equity products, which, in turn, could easily pit adviser interests against investor interests.

Behavioural economics has an explanation for this, too. It's called *self-serving bias*, which is completely aligned with traditional economics. Generally, all things being equal, people tend to seek the highest reward if the same effort is required.

Putting relatively more money into a part of the world precisely because it is expensive and therefore makes up a larger portion of the world's economy than it ordinarily might is hardly an example of focus and discipline.

. . .

People can't credibly be perpetually bullish and also honest arbiters of market valuations and investor conduct. While obviously there are times when a bullish outlook is entirely justified, it's equally true that such a bullish outlook can sometimes be at odds with reality. Maintaining an optimistic stance no matter what the circumstances are can lead to very real problems. As a result, I fear for the near future. If at some point we experience a major drawdown the likes of which has not been experienced in our lifetimes, we'll all be in uncharted waters. For those of you who believe the resolve you displayed by hanging on in early 2020 is proof of the steely resolve you would likely display in a bigger downturn, kindly reconsider your confidence. You may be like Stockdale's GIs.

What happened in early 2020 was a blip. That drawdown lasted less than six weeks! It was easily the shortest *bear market* in history. If you were away on vacation for the first nine months of 2020, you could look at your 2019 year-end statement and then look at your Q3 2020 statement and be forgiven if you thought nothing much had happened. Your adviser might think they can keep you invested the next time the market takes a big drop, and you probably think you have the stomach for it, too. After all, you both survived the bear of 2020 — how hard could it be to survive another? But what if the next big drop is bigger than anything you ever imagined? As of the beginning of 2022, advisers are required to gather additional information about client attitudes surrounding a drop — taking into account both the depth of the drop and the duration. Regulators have never required this. Here are two examples of the questions:

> What is the approximate loss in a one-year period that you would be willing to accept before deciding to change investments?

o Less than 5 percent decline
o 5 percent to 10 percent decline
o 10 percent to 15 percent decline
o 15 percent to 25 percent decline
o 25 percent or more decline

Given the fluctuation of any investment portfolio, how long would you be willing to wait for the investments to regain any lost value?

o Less than 3 months
o 3 to 6 months
o 6 months to 1 year
o 1 to 2 years
o 2 or more years

If we experience a major drawdown, anyone who did not choose the last option on both questions is telling their adviser and their firm in writing that they would be inclined to sell if they had significant equity exposure.

• • •

I simply do not think the industry is ready for what might lie ahead. I do not think investors are ready, either. Basically, if we get hit by a genuine *bear market* akin to what was experienced in the 1930s, I believe neither advisers nor investors will be able to properly cope. I also think the financial planning being done is dangerously optimistic. It seems that some advisers and their clients have to come to terms with the very real possibility that returns could be significantly lower for the rest of their lives.

Chapter 8

Case Studies in Financial Planning

Investors may think their adviser's "the man"
Yet wear rose-coloured glasses when reviewing their plan

FINANCIAL PLANNING IS A KEY component of comprehensive advice. Unfortunately, some financial professionals don't do nearly as much as they should. Many of the excellent planners who do engage in the activity provide advice that is fanciful because they use assumptions that are wildly out of line with what is recommended by their governing body. In fact, the discrepancies between what planning organizations are recommending and what many practitioners are recommending is stark. The difference, many believe, is attributable to Bullshift. Projecting comfortable retirements is good for business.

This chapter delves into three specific areas where financial planning is affected by Bullshift: return assumptions, when to take Canada Pension Plan (the CPP), and the so-called implementation gap, which investigates the disconnect between what people say they will do and what they do. In all three cases, behaviour might be called into question — meaning that changed behaviour might very well lead to better outcomes if it can be identified and fixed early on.

• • •

Example 1: Return Assumptions

Annual planning assumptions guidelines are typically released in late April by the certification bodies that regulate the certified financial planner (CFP) designation. They use a complex methodology involving myriad inputs. Some of these inputs are historical, which is interesting, since the guidelines are meant to be forward-looking. Conspicuously and tellingly, however, they do not make any express reference to Shiller's CAPE work, even though it is among the most credible and reliable predictors of future returns. In fairness, some of the experts consulted in reaching the guideline assumptions use the Shiller work, but the final documents they produce typically make no direct reference to its applicability.

• • •

According to the 2022 assumptions guidelines published by FP Canada/ IQPF, reasonable return assumptions (all numbers before advisory fees and product costs) are as follows:

Borrowing Rate:	4.3 percent
Inflation Rate:	2.1 percent
Short-term Income:	2.3 percent
Fixed Income:	2.8 percent
Canadian Equity:	6.3 percent
Developed Equity:	6.6 percent
Emerging Equity:	7.7 percent

The guidelines permit a variance of 0.5 percent in either direction to allow for company policies and vagaries. While the guidelines are not explicit in illustrating how this should be interpreted, many feel this variance is best applied at the overall portfolio level. For instance, a portfolio that is 50 percent stocks and 50 percent bonds might assume stock returns that are 1 percent higher on average and bond returns that are 1 percent lower on average, but the blended portfolio return assumption would be unchanged and therefore compliant.

The certification bodies also make it clear that, to be right, it is both appropriate and necessary to reduce all return expectations by their associated fees. Fees can vary greatly but are the sum of both the product costs and payments for advice. Obviously, actual results will vary — possibly by a wide margin, even for the same asset allocation. Despite the clear admonition to include cost considerations in whatever projections are made, there is a deep-seated concern that some advisers do not, in fact, reduce their return assumptions to account for costs. The bodies that produce the guidelines do not audit projections to determine the rigour with which the guidelines are followed when planners generate projections for their clients, so no one can verify compliance with complete certainty. Rumours abound, but because of the lack of meaningful audit capacities, they can be neither reliably substantiated nor refuted.

This is the point where the obvious concern needs to be stated explicitly. It is likely that many financial plans in Canada today use return assumptions that are unreasonably high. That's a legitimate concern. The problem is threefold: some people ignore the recommendations and use their own higher numbers; the recommended numbers are themselves quite likely to be too high; and whatever numbers are used ought to be lowered by the fees and expenses incurred by the client.

Anyone who seriously thinks that it is "reasonable" to expect a 2.8 percent long-term return on investment-grade fixed income, for instance, is almost wilfully blind. The thirty-year yield on government bonds is less than that — and that's before product costs and the cost of advice! Later, we'll explore what many experts believe are more appropriate assumptions — and the implications for those (hint: much lower) assumptions for your retirement plans. For now, let's just deal with the more immediate problem.

Most people I talk to who make retirement planning projections use numbers that are markedly higher than what is being recommended. Given that it is nearly impossible to reliably determine what numbers most people are using, I'll begin with a disclaimer that what follows are likely reasonable guesses based on various conversations with people who do projections for their clients.

I have spoken with numerous practitioners who use numbers like 5 percent for a conservative portfolio, 6 percent for a balanced portfolio, and 7 percent for an aggressive portfolio. There are others that use higher numbers still. Despite these high assumption numbers, many call them "reasonable" and depict the numbers put forth by genuinely reasonable people as inappropriately low. In time, it will become abundantly clear that projections based on lower assumptions will be more accurate — and therefore more reasonable. In the meantime, there's some *cognitive dissonance* that screams for reconciliation. Here's a simple illustration from the guidelines:

Asset Class	Projected Return	Percent Allocation	Contribution to Total Return
Short-term	2.3 percent	5 percent	2.3 percent x 0.05 = 0.115 percent
Fixed Income	2.8 percent	45 percent	2.8 percent x 0.45 = 1.26 percent
Canadian Equity	6.3 percent	40 percent	6.1 percent x 0.40 = 2.52 percent
Developed Equity	6.6 percent	10 percent	6.6 percent x 0.10 = 0.66 percent
Totals		100 percent	4.555 percent

Basically, the expected return for a conservative, 50/50 portfolio (half stocks, half bonds) is about 4.5 percent. That's before fees, costs, and other expenses. Now, let's look at the impact of those expenses. If you're using a traditional broker who uses individual stocks and bonds to build your portfolio, there might be no product costs, but a fee of about 1.25 percent; if your adviser uses ETFs, those might cost about 0.25 percent on top of that same 1.25 percent fee; and if your adviser uses mutual funds, those funds might cost (i.e., have an average management expense ratio, or MER) of about 2.0 percent, on average. The MER is the annual cost of holding a fund. That may not sound like a lot, but it is hugely important.

One of my websites features a portfolio calculator that performs this exercise in simple dollars: standup.today/standup-investment-portfolio-calculator/.

The point here is that seemingly small differences in returns, costs, or both can have a truly staggering impact on your terminal wealth over the course of your lifetime. Accordingly, I would be remiss if I didn't at least mention two other options, if only for the sake of completeness. You could be a self-directed investor and pay only for products (typically 0.25 percent to 2.25 percent) or you could choose to work with a robo-adviser and pay something like 0.5 percent for robo-adviser services plus an additional 0.25 percent or so in product costs (0.75 percent total). In both cases, you might be paying less, but you would certainly not be getting financial planning work as part of the deal. The crucial point is that neither investment products nor advice is free. If charged separately, products typically cost between 0.15 percent and 1.5 percent and advisory fees between 1 percent and 1.25 percent. If bundled together, the total cost is typically between 1.5 percent and 2.5 percent.

The concerns here are transparency, disclosure, and financial literacy. The industry insists it believes in investor education, yet often does a less than stellar job of explaining the impacts associated with costs and fees. In all cases (self-directed, robo-advice, full advice), the expected return is about 4.5 percent before fees. After fees have been considered, something, again, that is necessary when doing planning properly, the expected total return is approximately 3.5 percent for the advice with a traditional securities account, 3.0 percent for the advice with an ETF account, and 2.25 percent for the advice with a mutual fund account. Remember that inflation should be assumed at 2 percent, so the total real return (i.e., after all expenses and above inflation) is extremely modest in all cases. Basically, the expected nominal return for a 50/50 portfolio should likely be between 2.25 percent and 3.5 percent and the expected real return (i.e., gain in purchasing power) would be only between 1.5 percent and 0.25 percent.

Looking at the three ways of using a model portfolio, let's take a point a bit higher than the middle and assume a 3 percent nominal return. Using the *rule of 72*, an investor would need to wait approximately twenty-four years before the money currently in their portfolio doubles. That's the hard reality of the world we live in.

Investors and planning clients want to be assured that they're going to be okay. Everyone, it seems, wants to avoid the inconvenient truth, so they opt for higher estimates. It would likely not surprise you to learn that there are many planners who are assuming a compounded annual return closer to 5 percent. Don't take my word for it. Ask the person you're working with to show their work and explain their assumptions. Once again, to compare, here's an example of what you might expect:

Portfolio Risk	Typical Assumption	Asset Mix
Low	5.0 percent	50 percent stocks, 50 percent bonds
Medium	6.0 percent	75 percent stocks, 25 percent bonds
High	7.0 percent	100 percent stocks

The total difference in this example may well be north of 2.0 percent. Remember, too, that inflation is quite properly assumed to be running at 2 percent in Canada but is actually quite a bit higher as we go to print. Accordingly, real returns (i.e., the returns after inflation) may be considerably lower still. Many advisers whose planning work is otherwise excellent simply do not consider the impact that cost can have on their clients' terminal wealth. At a minimum, some advisers certainly don't seem prepared to acknowledge it as a material factor in their clients' retirement projections. Those who use the lowest assumptions are likely more conservative and realistic. That is an adviser who does not resort to Bullshift to land an account.

Whether this adviser behaviour is deliberate or not is not even the question. Either way, the news is bad. Either advisers know they are fudging facts and best practices (i.e., they have questionable ethics) or they do not know they are fudging facts (i.e., they are unwittingly ignorant of how to apply the data). Either way, the outcomes are compromised. Investors absolutely need to ask their advisers about the assumptions being used in modelling their retirement projections. If they do not, I strongly suspect that many will ultimately find that their nest egg will be much, much smaller than they thought it would be. My guess is that a very large majority of people who are having projections run on their behalf will end up being much less wealthy than they thought they'd be, because their return assumptions are simply far too high to be credible.

There's a tool on my author website, standup.today, where you can plug in whatever return assumptions and fee assumptions you want, within

reason. You can use it to set reasonable return expectations to do simple, but customized, projections.

You need to understand that financial planners, like any professionals, want to be liked. Perhaps even more to the point, they want to attract new clients. Telling the truth can be a downer. There are a great many potential clients out there who would rather buy into industry Bullshift than plan while using reasonable assumptions based on their actual situation. Bullshift has persisted for this long because clients like it and find it comforting. In their minds, an overly optimistic adviser who promises a 6 percent return is often more desirable than a realistic adviser who properly projects a 3.5 percent return. That's simply not right. Some investors are complicit in the ongoing Bullshift because they prefer to be told comforting lies. They happily give their business to people who make optimistic promises rather than to people who make prudent, responsible, evidence-based recommendations based on industry-sanctioned best practices.

Financial advisers are not all the same. There are many extremely capable planners. Some advisers specialize and therefore know more about capital markets than they do about financial planning, so they farm that part of their role out. This can be the source of trouble. If advisers have been telling their clients that a 6 percent rate of return is both realistic and attainable, the advisers will want their financial plans and retirement illustrations to be written for their clients in a way that reflects that position. Corporate in-house planners are then put into a tight spot. They want to serve their adviser colleagues, but they are simultaneously required to comply with regulatory guidelines. The two demands are often irreconcilable. You absolutely need to ask about the assumptions used when you get projections from your adviser.

• • •

There are many experts who believe that the long-term historical (and future) difference in the rate of return between stocks and bonds (sometimes called a "risk premium") is about 5 percent or a bit less. For discussion purposes, let's say 7 percent for equity (stocks) and 2 percent for income (bonds). The numbers are generally close to that range, anyway. As such, a 50/50 portfolio has an expected pre-cost return of 4.5 percent.

Alternatively, since the FP Canada/IQPF Guidelines suggest a blended average risk premium of only 3.2 percent, some people might suggest that to move to the more traditional risk premium, we'd need to either lower return expectations for income or raise return expectations for equity or do a bit of both. If done judiciously, the outcome may well be very similar to what is recommended, even though the calculation would be quite different. Most people have a balanced portfolio that consists of something close to two-thirds stocks and one-third bonds. If the 1.8 percent gap between the prescribed risk premium and the historically accepted risk premium were to be reconciled by lowering return expectations for bonds by 1.2 percent, while simultaneously raising the return expectations for stocks by 0.6 percent, the total blended return for the two-thirds/one-third portfolio would be unchanged if everything else was the same. Different approaches, same outcome.

There are some who believe that in a post-Covid world, it might be reasonable to modify all assumptions further downward given the slower economic growth that virtually all experts agree we are in for. The "wow" factor — as in, "Is that all I'll get?" — will be even more pronounced once costs are incorporated into the calculations.

• • •

Because proper planning requires that the assumed return for any given asset class or blended portfolio return should subtract the cost of products and advice, the matter of cost is brought into sharp focus. To illustrate, suppose we look at a traditional 60/40 portfolio (60 percent stocks and 40 percent income). Even with stocks earning 7 percent (x 0.6 = 4.2 percent) and bonds earning 2 percent (x 0.4 = 0.8 percent), the expected return for the pre-cost portfolio is only 5.0 percent in total. Now, imagine if the investor used mutual funds that cost 2.5 percent to build their portfolio. They'd be putting up all the money, taking all the risk ... and getting only half the annual return!

PART II

. . .

This might also be a good opportunity to discuss the prognosis for inflation. Nobody knows what the future holds. Here's what we know about the past: since the early 1980s, interest rates have dropped from the high teens to essentially zero. Despite this, in the early 1990s, the central banks set their targets for inflation at 2 percent (± 1 percent) and inflation has almost always stayed within that range. Until 2021. For more than a generation, we supplemented what would have otherwise been anemic economic growth with additional monetary stimulus.

If, down the road, inflation can go back down to about 2 percent a year, we can return to the old paradigm, but only for a short while. In the context of an interest rate environment that has seen a steady annual decline of about forty basis points (0.4 percent) for nearly forty years without any inflation, what do you suppose might happen if the current bout of inflation was brought under control and future rates literally could not go lower? Looking back, it seems likely that for over a generation we have achieved price stability despite prolonged, repeated rate cuts. With no more room to cut, how will central banks stimulate in the future?

What's needed is a sort of "goldilocks" monetary policy — interest rates that are not too high and not too low. Keeping inflation in check while supporting economic growth is a contemporary challenge unlike any in history. Even if policy makers were to succeed in keeping inflation at 2 percent, modest returns mean the after-inflation gains will be minuscule. Putting it all together, we have a near-term future that features lower-than-expected returns being eroded by fees and costs. Making everything especially challenging is the impact of inflation.

If one were to start with $100,000 earning 4 percent and growing over thirty years, it would yield a modest $331,500, but at 2 percent (after costs), it would yield a paltry $182,350. The impact of costs would be so dramatic that it would eat away nearly $150,000 which, in turn, would represent nearly half this person's wealth in retirement. Here's a number for you to consider: $547,500. If you consider the expenses of a couple (aged sixty-five) from the time of their retirement until they both turn ninety, that number represents the cost of their meals alone. Twenty-five years × two people × three meals a day × $10 a meal over 365 days a year gets you to $547,500. Let's look at what happens if we choose an aggressive, low-cost portfolio that earns 6 percent. For that to be possible, the allocation toward stocks would have to be close to 100 percent and the cost would have to be quite modest. Still, the retirement date value in that scenario is $602,258! The difference could literally be life-altering. If inflation is also pegged at 2 percent, that 4 percent return not only drops to 2 percent after costs and fees — it drops to zero when accounting for inflation!

I'm not saying anyone should be more aggressive simply to make progress. Again, the best portfolio is the one you can stick with. I'm simply saying that the combination of lower-than-previous returns, coupled with the real possibility of higher-than-previous inflation, volatility, and costs means people will almost certainly need to reset their expectations.

Many people are staring at projections that assume returns anywhere from 1 percent to 3 percent higher than what they will likely experience. This will not end well. The people who buy into Bullshift will one day need to cope with one or more of the following:

o   retiring later — perhaps even a lot later than they origin-
    ally thought
o   retiring with far less than they thought they'd have
o   accepting a quality of life that is a poor replica of what they
    enjoyed while working

The warm, fuzzy feelings that accompany projections made while looking through rose-coloured glasses can give way to cold shivers of dread when the real picture is revealed. Why is it that so many of us are so easily led astray? Why is it that so many of us would give our life savings to someone who makes reassuring promises rather than to someone who diligently goes about their work with prudence, conservatism, and a responsible attitude? In general, people say that they prefer to do business with the following types of people:

o people they like (some advisers focus on being likeable more than on being diligent)
o people who keep their word (but clients can't discern who these people might be, since it's not possible to know what the future will be when they engage an adviser)
o people who have their best interests at heart
o people who are honest, ethical, and have high integrity

Rolling the Dice

Investors grappling with lower interest rates have to take bigger risks if they want to equal returns of two decades ago.

Estimates of what investors needed to earn 7.5%

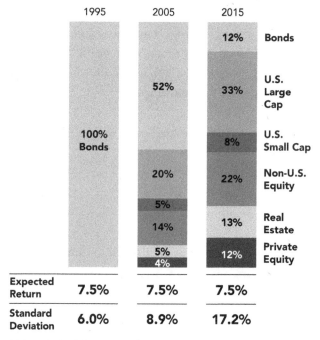

	1995	2005	2015	
			12%	Bonds
		52%	33%	U.S. Large Cap
	100% Bonds		8%	U.S. Small Cap
		20%	22%	Non-U.S. Equity
		5%	13%	Real Estate
		14%		
		5%	12%	Private Equity
		4%		
Expected Return	**7.5%**	**7.5%**	**7.5%**	
Standard Deviation	**6.0%**	**8.9%**	**17.2%**	

*Likely amount by which returns could vary
Source: Callan Associates (*Wall Street Journal*)

In one generation, the amount of risk required to generate the same 7.5% return grew more than twofold. Today, that return isn't even attainable using traditional asset classes and reasonable assumptions.

In the end, though, people seem to be hard-wired to prefer working with nice salespeople rather than diligent professionals — even when they insist they want the professional approach. How many advisers spend time thinking about how they might offer advice that is conservative and evidence-based, but also nuanced enough to consider circumstances? For planning purposes, optimism is good, but realism is better.

Here's a way to illustrate the trend of needing to take more risk just to get the same (or perhaps even lower) return going forward. Callan Associates has shown how in one short generation, portfolio construction has become more complex, expensive, and (especially) risky just to get a 7.5 percent return. Note that these numbers are historical. Based on the assumption guidelines noted earlier, the only likely way to get to 7.5 percent would be to have a portfolio that consists entirely of emerging market equity and private equity. In fact, a 7.5 percent return may not be possible in the future — under any circumstances!

Example 2: When to Take CPP Benefits

Based on current life expectancies, a large majority of Canadians would be better off if they waited before electing to receive government entitlements such as the CPP. The statistics show, however, that few Canadians choose to do so. Research done for the FP Canada Research Foundation shows that most Canadians elect to take their CPP entitlements on or before their sixty-fifth birthday, which is a sort of over/under threshold based on the calculation of those benefits. The program is designed so that people are effectively penalized for taking benefits prior to their sixty-fifth birthday and rewarded for waiting until after their sixty-fifth birthday to begin collecting. The applied financial evidence shows that most of these same people would be better off if they waited. What's going on here?

For most of us, the only rational reason for electing to take government entitlements early is if you honestly think you're going to die early. Anyone who makes it to about age eighty-one will receive more money by waiting as long as possible (i.e., their seventieth birthday) before receiving a government pension. But most people ignore this fact. Again, the question is why?

The problem, it seems, is that most people are overly confident of their ability to generate higher returns with discretionary investments than through longstanding national programs that offer government guarantees. Let's consider that point. Depending on the geographical location of your equity investments, the assumed rate of return is typically somewhere between 6 percent and 7 percent. Meanwhile, the penalty for taking CPP earlier is 0.6 percent per month (7.2 percent annualized) and the benefit of waiting until over age sixty-five is 0.7 percent per month (8.4 percent annualized). Where else can an investor get returns that are likely to be better than one would expect in equity markets with absolutely no market risk whatsoever? The responsible answer is obvious: unless you're extremely fortunate and extremely willing to take risk, you simply can't.

There are certainly many people who make the decision to begin receiving CPP on or before their sixty-fifth birthday entirely on their own. There are at least two possible reasons why this might be:

1. Benign ignorance of evidence
2. Bullshift

The second possibility is that if a client needs (say) $36,000 in annual living expenses and that money can come either entirely from their RRIF or $12,000 from CPP entitlements and $24,000 from the RRIF, there might be more going on in the decision-making. Specifically, there could also be a psychological reason. Some people prefer keeping as much money as possible in their discretionary retirement plans because it feels good. This is something called the *wealth effect*. Some people feel wealthier simply because their statements show a larger number — even if the total amount received in their lifetimes would have been greater had they chosen the alternative route.

Finally, there's Bullshift. Many advisers could honestly believe, despite the recommendations and guidelines mentioned earlier, that they can reliably earn more than 8.4 percent a year for their clients.

Recently, a new product called the Purpose Longevity Fund was released to a moderate amount of fanfare and with a significant marketing budget. Hailed as a breakthrough in retirement income planning, the product is a hybrid between a traditional mutual fund and an annuity. Clients are pooled into cohorts born within the same three-year window for purposes of risk-sharing. These clients then get a balanced portfolio that pays a set amount (a little over 6 percent a year at age sixty-five) for as long as the client stays alive. The longer one stays alive, the longer the payments keep coming. Since one of the greatest financial risks inhabitants of developed nations are likely to face is outliving their principal, you'd think people would be beating a path to use the product, which is the first of its kind to address longevity risk and does so in much the same way as delaying government benefits.

Example 3: Overcoming the Implementation Gap

Even the best-laid plans can go awry. Notwithstanding the concerns above about planning assumptions and when to take CPP, there are several things advisers can do to add real value for their clients. But then the problem is not whether the advice is good, but whether the clients can be persuaded to take it. Even the very best advice is useless if it is not acted on. This is where the rubber hits the road regarding behaviour modification. Many fields of endeavour suffer from the say/do challenge, where people say one thing, but consistently do something else. Think of how many patients don't take their medication — much to the consternation of their family doctors. Life just gets in the way, it seems.

Another bit of research completed for the FP Canada Research Foundation was completed by a company called BE Works, which was founded by best-selling author Dan Ariely. It offers research and consulting services to various corporations and organizations that want to apply the principles of *behavioural economics* in their processes and recommendations in the hopes of achieving better outcomes. In a 2020 paper entitled "Applying Behavioural Economics to Tackle the Implementation Gap," the company made numerous recommendations.

BE Works points out that most business problems can be boiled down to two questions: "How do people make decisions?" and "How can we encourage certain decisions over others?" Applying the scientific method to their work plan, they made several observations and offered some potential remedies. They cited research showing that stated intentions predict behaviour only 28 percent of the time. This might cause one to question the value of most marketing research that asks consumers about their attitudes toward products and services, then uses the answers to predict purchasing behaviour.

BE Works, dealing exclusively with CFP professionals, determined that many plans used disparate discovery methods and often missed a call to action (i.e., "What do I do with this?"). There was also a curious observation that was counterintuitive: a *licensing effect*. Ironically, many clients felt as though they essentially "had things under control" simply because they had had a plan written for them — even if they often did nothing to implement the details of that plan! Basically, people were acting as though the process of merely writing the plan was the big life-changing deliverable, rather than rolling up their sleeves and implementing the recommendations in the plan itself once they had received it.

A survey was used to test hypotheses and prioritize possible sequential areas of intervention:

Awareness	Do clients recognize the need for a financial plan?
Perception	Do they understand the benefit of having one?
Evaluation	What are client attitudes toward the plan?
Decision	Do clients form plans of action?
Action	Does behaviour follow the stated intention?
Maintenance	Do actions continue, or do they stop?

It is precisely at the point between decision and action that the say/do gap exists. Several factors can potentially derail the implementation of the plan. For instance, there's the *social desirability bias*, which can cause people to be less than forthcoming with some of the more embarrassing elements of their financial lives. You know the saying, "garbage in, garbage out"? Well, any plan is only as good as the factor inputs used in writing it. If those inputs are less than accurate due to client embarrassment, it follows that the resulting plans will most likely be inaccurate.

It was determined that the main reasons for the say/do gap are procrastination and a lack of goal-framing. Specific challenges regarding decision making included inertia, *status quo bias*, and the *licensing effect*. Meanwhile, the challenges for the action-taking phase included a lack of urgency and a lack of future self-connection. Interestingly, the survey found no link between the length of time clients worked with their CFP professional and the degree of implementation reported.

Other potential drivers of client action were found to be similarly unimportant in explaining the level of engagement. These included the quality of the relationship between the client and the CFP, client trust in the planner, and understanding the value of planning. This should not be an indication that those elements are unimportant. It seems many people chose not to implement many recommendations *despite* having strong relationships featuring high levels of trust.

The *licensing effect* is especially interesting because it provides a psychological excuse for suboptimal behaviour — like joining a gym, but never going. It appears going through the process and receiving a written, clear, and actionable plan is rewarding in and of itself. People may then feel they have a licence to not follow through on the plan's recommendations.

Procrastination is another problem. Much of this challenge can be met head-on at the point of plan delivery. Precommitment is an obvious way of overcoming the challenge. Getting clients to precommit (in writing, if possible) to acting on the recommendations and behaviours found in the plan before the plan is even presented to them can go a long way in ensuring that purposeful actions are taken and habits developed.

PART II

Observations

Former Bank of Canada Governor Stephen Poloz has posited that there are five major "tectonic forces" impacting our economy today. Taken together, they paint a clear picture of the public policy challenges our politicians face, as well as of the intellectual recalibration we all need to make to properly consider the structural changes that lie ahead.

The first major force is population aging. Not only are we living longer, but our children are having fewer children, so there are more people retiring and fewer people working. That's a major drag on productivity and economic growth and it will continue for generations to come.

The second major force is the role of debt. Governments have tried to prevent (or possibly just delay and lessen the effects of) a recession by issuing public debt. Meanwhile, private debt is at record levels and (stop me if you've heard this before) that acts as a drag on both economic growth and the returns we are likely to see in capital markets. According to the International Monetary Fund, global debt surpassed global gross domestic product for the first time in 2020. Not a good trend. Meanwhile, household debt is at record levels all over the world — even as we experienced a massive bull run in 2020 and 2021.

The third major force is a positive one: technology. Digitalization and artificial intelligence, among other factors, have gone a long way toward keeping our economy strong. As the role technology plays in the economy increases, however, there is a concern that many jobs will be outsourced to ever more intelligent and capable iterations of these technologies. Self-driving trucks could put a small army of truckers out of business in a few years. Sometime after that, doctors, lawyers, and even financial advisers may see their careers being undercut by new technology. That, in turn, can have major implications for employment policy.

The fourth major force is the march toward greater inequality. Some say this is about income, but others will point out that it is about assets. Those that have had things in the past tend to have even more things in the future. Pre-existing wealth begets the accumulation of further wealth. That, in turn, fuels populism, disrespect for "those in charge" — and increasing likelihood that desperate times will lead to desperate measures.

Finally, there's climate change. The threat of this has resulted in the rush to decarbonize our economies. Already, we have had to deal with massive floods, devastating hurricanes, rampant wildfires, and the loss of arable farmland; in the future, there is the real possibility of having literally millions of climate-related refugees nomadically looking for a place to call home. All of these things come at a significant cost.

There are many who think a sixth force has recently emerged. Vladimir Putin's cynical and maniacal attack on Ukraine in February 2022 has essentially cancelled the so-called peace dividend that had been paying out for over thirty years. Countries that would have otherwise spent money on business development are now being forced to divert some of those resources into military procurement and refurbishing.

Many people who profess to be active proponents of financial planning are likely not taking these undeniable trends into account. In failing to do so, they may unwittingly be engaging in Bullshift, because their narratives lack a proper consideration of the changes taking place right before our eyes. Economic growth needs to exceed interest rates for us to have any chance at meaningful prosperity.

. . .

While there is a large body of research regarding *behavioural economics* generally, there's also a small but growing body of research that can be applied to financial planning considerations. The evidence for overly optimistic planning assumptions appears to be widespread. The evidence for people taking CPP relatively early and not following through on written planning recommendations is widely available, but there are still many questions. Why, exactly, are so many people making so many irrational decisions when there's clear and compelling evidence to point them in the right direction? Even when the problems are well understood, there are challenges in getting clients to act in their own self-interest.

It appears we've stumbled upon a missing link in the business of offering financial advice to retail clients. Too often, advisers have dedicated themselves to things like ratios, trends, valuations, asset allocations, taxes, and the like. Those matters are self-evidently important, but it may very well be that other considerations — matters that receive scarce attention in comparison — are even more important. Individual and group behaviour, rational decision-making, and the pervasive biases that we all have get relatively little consideration in modern adviser training.

If the studies that suggest there's considerable value in behavioural coaching are correct, then it logically follows that we ought to be doing more to teach advisers so that they, in turn, can coach their clients toward better behaviours and outcomes.

Chapter 9

———

How the Government Entrenches Bullshift

Similarities between advisers and politicians have been detected:
One wants to manage your nest egg, the other to get elected.

THERE ARE TOO MANY CONSPIRACY theories out there already. This chapter is not about secret plots, invasions of privacy, or restrictions of freedoms. Rather, it is about the eerie similarity between how politicians and financial advisers speak to the public. What they project. Why they project it. Humans are both rational and emotional. In politics and in finance, we form our opinions for mostly emotional reasons, then use faulty reasoning to support those opinions.

• • •

When the global pandemic first hit, both the economy and markets went into a free fall, but the solution to the economic drop would prove to create a new set of problems. In the aftermath of previous, similar crises, governments had had a chance to look back on their decisions to see if there might not be better ways of doing things should similar situations arise in the future. To the credit of publicly elected officials, lessons were learned, and new approaches were taken.

In the years after the Great Depression that began in 1929, governments implemented policies that backfired — they actively made things worse. These included both severe austerity measures and high tariffs. These days, it is widely accepted that the policy response to the Great Depression exacerbated the situation. Well-intended actions had unintended consequences, causing people to hunker down and look inward.

More recently, beginning in the months near the end of the Global Financial Crisis of 2007 to 2009, governments embarked on a series of previously untried monetary policies designed to offer a massive infusion of liquidity to drive down interest rates. This was done to stabilize markets and stimulate growth. Known in policy circles as *quantitative easing*, the approach involved large purchases of bonds and other securities by central banks. Stabilizing the financial sector was critical, because it encouraged lending, which in turn would ultimately allow consumers to spend and businesses to invest with confidence. Unlike the response in the 1930s, the public response to the more recent crisis was highly successful.

There were concerns, however. Given the unusually low interest rates put in place in the aftermath of *quantitative easing*, governments around the world signalled a desire to "normalize" rates — they wanted to bring them up off the floor to more traditional levels. The low-interest policy was instituted to provide temporary respite from a global crisis. It was never intended to be permanent. Some people were spooked about what normalization might entail. The problem was dubbed the "taper tantrum." Commentators rightly feared that markets would crumble if the easy-money programs ceased.

More recently still, a global pandemic caused governments around the Western world to put their economies into publicly supported and government-induced comas of sorts by ordering shops, offices, schools, and churches to be closed temporarily while public health experts and epidemiologists worked feverishly to better understand the true nature of this largely unknown enemy.

As with the Global Financial Crisis, monetary policy came swiftly to the rescue, only this time with the added kicker of stimulus. Since a large percentage of the population was temporarily unemployed in many nations, fiscal policy (how governments tax and spend) was also employed extensively. Deficits soared. By the summer of 2020, stores and schools began to reopen and society got used to the idea of wearing masks and "social distancing" in public. The economy was on the comeback trail.

By the end of 2020, however, the pandemic was worsening by the week. A new set of shutdowns was being imposed and the previously announced supports were not only extended but enhanced. In an economic update issued at that time, the Canadian government promised to do whatever was necessary to keep Canadians safe while Covid-19 was stalking our streets and nursing homes. Public support for these measures, while not universal, was widespread. The leader of the Opposition even said they would provide the same level of support if they were in the prime minister's shoes. In terms of rescuing the economy while keeping its citizens safe, the government's response to the pandemic was seen to have been successful.

Financial advisers and governments can both be Bullshifters. A couple of chapters ago, we looked at how things evolved from adviser and investor perspectives. Now, let's look at it from the perspective of the people devising the policies.

Governments were determined to keep the good times rolling. Some people might believe that the government's actions were a cynical attempt to manipulate the business cycle, or forward-looking economic management, or Bullshift, or some combination of factors, but the intervention was clearly designed to maintain a positive outlook. In the end, it mostly worked, and people mostly supported the moves. That is true whether talking about media, public health experts, investors, or advisers. There were those who opposed certain measures, to be sure, but the opposition was mostly rooted in libertarian dogma. In the early twenty-first century, there are not many true fiscal conservatives left anywhere in political circles.

There were, however, some rather pronounced and unintended consequences. As in the Global Financial Crisis, rates during the pandemic were once again at rock-bottom lows. This time, however, the low rates were accompanied by both an unprecedented amount of government spending and a declaration by central banks that they were willing to consider revising their mandates to recalibrate their inflation targets, allowing their economies to "run hot" temporarily while people returned to work. The phrase "lower for longer" became a part of our lexicon as central bankers began to set the expectation of not normalizing for a decade or longer.

The central bankers were adamant there would be no taper tantrums in the 2020s when the pandemic abated. Not only were people confident about the current environment, but they also believed that, in the immediate aftermath of the pandemic, public policy makers would provide cover for the foreseeable future as well. Flush with the confidence that both governments and central bankers "had their backs," investors began taking outsized risks.

The short, sharp recession and *bear market* was a unique phenomenon of the first half of 2020. It was old news. A blip. A footnote in the middle of a long-running *bull market*. By the end of 2020, many of those receiving government support had returned to the labour force. Stock markets revisited old highs and resumed an upward trajectory. Once it became obvious that central bankers and politicians were going to do "whatever it takes," as the president of the European Central Bank, Mario Draghi, said, investor confidence returned with a vengeance. The Bullshift trade was on. As soon as the investing public realized that policy makers were going "all in" on an economic recovery, they in turn felt they had a green light to go "all in."

Self-Serving Bias

A concept that is well known but seldom discussed in the field of finance is *self-serving bias* and its first cousin, *attribution bias*. This is when a person takes credit for positive events or outcomes yet blames outside factors for negative events or outcomes: heads, I'm smart; tails, I'm unlucky.

A *self-serving bias* is any cognitive or perceptual process that is distorted by the need to maintain and enhance self-esteem, or the tendency to perceive oneself in an overly favourable manner. Basically, it's bias that results in the misguided beliefs we hold about ourselves and others to make ourselves feel good and look good. Almost everyone tends to ascribe success to their own abilities and efforts but to ascribe failure to external factors. Which is just another way of saying we're all human.

We often reject negative feedback, focus on our strengths and achievements, and overlook our faults and failures. Some of us might be prone to take more responsibility in group work than to give credit to others. This also serves to protect our need for approbation and esteem. It's normal — but it's not healthy or constructive. Attributing failure externally can happen when the perception of a low probability of improvement takes hold.

Individuals low in self-awareness might attribute failure externally. In contrast, people with high self-awareness are more willing to be accountable for their thoughts and actions. They are more likely to attribute failure internally when there's room for improvement. It takes a certain amount of willingness to eat humble pie to admit you could be better. It also takes a commitment to self-improvement and change. Lots of people say they want to be better at things, just as lots of people make New Year's resolutions to lose weight. The thing is, actions speak louder than words. Lots of people will insist they want change but are simultaneously unwilling to change themselves.

Think back to the end of October 2020. The world had just gone through a nerve-wracking nine months. The only reason the market drawdown and short recession of earlier that year were not more severe and prolonged was that governments and central banks had offered the one-two punch of both fiscal and monetary stimulus. These were supposed to be temporary fixes. This stimulus did prevent a more immediate long-term recession, and stock markets did hit new highs (though mostly, it should be noted, because of higher valuations rather than higher earnings), and public debt and private debt reached unprecedented levels. Objectively speaking, things had gotten worse, yet people were feeling life was good.

With this zeitgeist as the backdrop, financial advisers were faced with two possible scenarios and two choices of recommendation for each:

o   The market continues to rebound and the adviser counsels
    to stay the course.

o The market continues to rebound and the adviser counsels to play defence.

o The market softens and the adviser counsels to stay the course.

o The market softens and the adviser counsels to play defence.

None of these courses of action was unambiguously correct. There were simply several options. Several related smaller decisions that stemmed from the original large decision would need to be made no matter how events unfolded. In all cases, the adviser had a mandate to do what they felt was best, using imperfect information based on a balance of probabilities that considered not only the likelihood of various things happening, but also the magnitude of the consequences associated with those things.

Pascal's Wager, a Vaccine, and a Portfolio Hedge

Much decision-making revolves around weighing competing options in a world where myriad outcomes are possible and where such things as probability, degree, and inherent uncertainty are all factors to be considered. In the political world, the number of things to be considered is seemingly limitless and the consequences are very high. With individuals, the stakes are smaller, but more immediate. In all cases, there's a Dirty Harry type of "Do you feel lucky, punk?" analysis that goes on — and often potentially life-altering decisions must be made in what can seem a split second.

There's an example from the history books that will help to illustrate the risk/return tradeoff between two alternatives. It's called Pascal's Wager. In the seventeenth century, a young French philosopher named Blaise Pascal suggested that a rational person should absolutely believe in God and live as though God exists. The stakes, Pascal said, were no less than a choice between an afterlife featuring an eternity of bliss and an afterlife featuring an eternity of perdition. Although he likely didn't think this at the time, the thought exercise may have represented the beginning of what are now the contemporary fields of *probability theory*, *decision theory*, and *pragmatism*.

It should be noted that the wager is presumptively Christian and mono-theistic. It works only if there is just one God; logic and thoroughness require that we acknowledge that the assumptions used in Pascal's model do not necessarily apply to the metaphor that follows.

Given the presumptively high stakes and the inherent uncertainty of the outcome due to the simple fact that the premise of the wager could not be verified either way, the proposition was spelled out roughly as follows: God either exists or not and you must decide on whether you believe in God. Since there are only two obvious alternatives to the two questions, the wagerer is left with four possible outcomes:

1. God exists and you believe.
2. God exists and you do not believe.
3. God does not exist, and you believe.
4. God does not exist, and you do not believe.

Options 3 and 4 carry no afterlife consequences whatsoever. If option 1 turns out to be true, however, then congratulations — you've just saved your eternal soul! Conversely, if option 2 turns out to be true, well, you can always hope that God is merciful and understanding.

Here's where it gets interesting. The identical exercise can be applied, in principle at least, to other decisions in the here and now. One is the Covid-19 vaccine (you can take it or not; it either works or does not). Another is the use of a portfolio hedge against a market bubble popping (you can either put a hedge on or not; the presumptive market bubble will either pop or it will not). Let's briefly compare the basic wager as it relates to bubbles and vaccines. Pay attention to how the logic applies to both government actions and the actions of advisers and individuals. In early 2021, the options were essentially as follows:

1. God exists and you believe.
   Vaccine works and you take it.
   Bubble bursts and you hedge against it.

2. God exists and you don't believe.
   Vaccine works and you don't take it.
   Bubble bursts and you don't hedge against it.

3. God doesn't exist and you believe.
   Vaccine doesn't work and you take it.
   Bubble doesn't burst and you hedge.

4. God doesn't exist and you don't believe.
   Vaccine doesn't work and you don't take it.
   Bubble doesn't burst and you don't hedge.

I have a friend who likes to say that "market timing is hard." I agree. As such, the use of a hedge against a market drawdown (at any time, in any situation) might be portrayed as some form of market timing, not as risk management.

What about the discernment of valuation levels? Is that hard, too? Most people, I suspect, would say that discerning valuation levels is easier, but still difficult to do anything meaningful with. Most would agree that it is easy to determine when markets are pricey but harder to come up with a scheme to monetize that assessment. Still, if something is difficult to do, does that mean we should not even attempt to do it?

The answer to that question might depend on the extent to which you concern yourself with *self-serving bias* and are prone to judging decisions by their outcomes rather than by the veracity of the thought processes used in leading up to the decision. Think about Pascal's Wager and what it might mean for things like reputational risk. If an adviser tells a client to stay the course and markets go up, or if an adviser counsels to play defence and markets go down, it is easy to look back after things become clear and say, "I told you so," or maybe even, "I knew it all along." Meanwhile, if that adviser counsels to stay the course and markets drop, or to play defence and markets continue to climb purposefully, that adviser is susceptible to criticism as a "bad adviser" who either "should have seen it coming" or who "engaged in reckless market timing." Errors of omission seem to be easier to forgive (from a client's perspective) or to explain away (from an adviser's) than errors of commission.

An unfavourable result can give way to *attribution bias*. People look for reasons to justify why and how their careful analysis failed to yield positive results when implemented. The concept of reputational risk needs to be considered, too. If you're "wrong," but do what everyone else does, it is unlikely you will be punished for your lack of appropriate responsiveness. After all, everyone else in the business is equally culpable. Similarly, if you're "right" while doing what everyone else does, you're just giving advice that is standard, common, and unexceptional. Note that the words *wrong* and *right* have been put in quotation marks. That's because the terms are really misnomers. Few decisions are unequivocally right or wrong. It's just that some work out and others don't. Sometimes a diamond; sometimes a stone.

Advisers indulge in groupthink and *herding* like anyone else might. Surrendering to these biases provides them with safety if they are wrong, which is critical because nobody really knows what's coming anyway. The narrative that they are anticipating is, "If it was so easy to see in advance, then why didn't anyone else take precautionary actions?" That somewhat rhetorical question misses the point. No one can reliably predict the future of market moves. That by itself, however, does not mean that alternative outcomes cannot be anticipated — or at least contemplated.

Probabilities can be calculated. Decision-trees can be employed. In fact, most business schools teach that the proper thing for any manager to do is to prepare for a wide range of possible circumstances and to react purposefully when one of the challenges presents itself. Just because you don't know exactly what will happen doesn't excuse you from preparing for what might happen.

Of course, having a plan is of no consequence if you are not willing to execute it. When and how does one act to guard against a downturn that comes when a valuation bubble pops? What plan do advisers have to deal with valuations that are at generational highs and interest rates that are at all-time lows, and both are likely to revert to their previous mid-point levels?

Recognizing that the last two factors are related (i.e., that low rates drive valuations up as investors are prepared to increase exposure to high-risk assets considering the poor returns offered by low-risk assets), are we to simply carry on as if nothing was unusual? If yes, then planning for a reckoning is useless. If no, then what exactly might the plan look like, what would it entail, and when would we know to spring into action?

. . .

Governments know the correlation between low rates and high valuations as well as individuals do. It is absolutely natural for the party in power to want the good times to continue at least until the next election. Although central bankers are supposed to operate independently and at arm's length, there's a growing body of anecdotal evidence that mandate creep has made its way into their implicitly revised job description so that central bankers are as willing to actively prolong business cycles and market expansions as they are to promote price stability. Whether you're the government of the day, an investor, or an adviser, the incentive to keep the good times rolling is a strong one. Governments and advisers can have a symbiotic relationship when it comes to normalizing Bullshift.

Everyone wins if the good times keep rolling, and people will take increasingly extraordinary measures to keep them rolling. In the end, when even extraordinary measures run into the limits of efficacy (such as inflation at almost forty-year highs), something has to give. If everyone goes along with bubbles getting ever bigger without protecting themselves, it logically follows that no one will be ready when those bubbles (deliberately plural) burst.

Rather than indulging in hyperactive, forecast-based market timing activity, what's needed is thoughtful, circumstance-based portfolio manipulation. Even if we all agree that no one can reliably time markets, does that mean that we should not even attempt to prepare ourselves in advance when the likelihood of bursting bubbles seems heightened? The question is a bit rhetorical, but not entirely. Even if a definitive answer is impossible to provide, simply asking the question can get the juices flowing.

How, exactly, should that type of proactive contingency behaviour be characterized? When an adviser wants to respond to high valuations but cannot do so without cries of "market timer!" levied against them, good intentions can give way to inertia — if only to fit in with peers. The opposite approach could be damning, too. Critics will say that it's not enough to have forecasted rain when trying to save clients from the deluge. Did the adviser build an ark?

Being nimble and reactive doesn't mean you're looking to call a top or a bottom, it means you're mindful of the environment you're operating in and prepared to take steps if necessary. It does not mean you're itching to do something simply because you've prepared yourself. Doing nothing if markets don't start tumbling is likely sensible conduct under the circumstances.

There are several things that might be done. These include the following:

o Ask to retake a risk assessment profile and then update your accounts to make them more conservative on the basis that your risk capacity or tolerance has been reduced. For an adviser, doing this pre-emptively is somewhat unorthodox from a compliance perspective but is entirely justifiable in certain circumstances — such as if the client has experienced a material life change.

o Rebalance your portfolio to the target mix. A prescription of 60 percent stocks, 40 percent bonds that has become unbalanced might be tapered back to 60/40. If you want to be especially cautious, you could even move all the way down to 50/50 and still be considered onside since a 10-percent variance from the prescribed mix is allowed.

o Move the stocks or bonds to other securities in the same asset class that may be less expensive from a valuation perspective or less volatile. Value stocks on the equity side; shorter term or higher credit quality on the income side.

o Diversify equities into other sectors, more holdings, or other geographic regions. Reduce concentration risk. Compared to developed markets, emerging market stocks have lower valuations, which leads to higher expected returns — all while being potentially better diversifiers.

o   Move some money into alternative assets that are at least less correlated with movements in fixed income and equity markets.

What's needed, it seems, is an environment in which advisers can use their discretion responsibly without fear of recriminations from their compliance department, their peers, or their clients. Obviously, oversight and controls are necessary. Giving advisers carte blanche is going too far in the opposite direction. Still, there needs to be some balance between being unduly prescriptive and being a reactive adviser who makes big decisions with other people's life savings based on gut feels and whatever news item hits their inbox that morning. What's needed is a culture of psychological safety. This involves admitting that there are alternative approaches and explanations to vexing problems, so everyone involved should check their *self-serving bias* at the door. Negative outcomes should not be pilloried if people can show their work.

Real psychological safety is only possible when one is able to demonstrate one's beliefs and opinions without fear of negative consequences. Those consequences could be felt in a person's self-image, status, or career relationships — with clients and coworkers alike. It's about removing fear from human interaction and replacing it with respect and permission. People should not feel sheepish about making mistakes or expressing unpopular viewpoints. Rather, divergent views should be welcomed and perhaps even celebrated, provided they are brought forward in good faith.

The conversations that some advisers have with their clients are at times overly optimistic. These conversations should favour realism. Too often, clients are only too willing to give their business to the adviser who has the most optimistic outlook about future lifestyles that are deemed to be plausible in the eyes of the client. Frank, comprehensive discussions about potential hard times ahead are sometimes bad for business. Advisers may pretend the future will be bright and clients may choose to believe them. The financial services industry is not alone in this approach. The same is true of governments.

Government Interaction with Voters

Governments have a responsibility to manage the economy, not the stock market. These are very different things, although you might not know it by how public policy is promoted. The two concepts are undeniably inter-related. We are living in a world where newly conventional levers have the intended consequence of rescuing the economy, while also having the po-tentially unintended consequence of manufacturing asset bubbles. To their credit, governments were purposeful and effective in meeting their initial objectives. Those objectives were focused squarely on the broad economy. The two concerns are broadly similar, but governments focus on big-picture, "macro" concerns, while individuals focus on personal-pocketbook, "micro" issues, where the phrase "what's in it for me" might be prominent.

While there are many ways one might explain the distinction between the economy and capital markets, here are three simple illustrations of how they differ and how the interaction between government intervention and public behaviour can be mutually reinforcing:

FOMO

The "fear of missing out" is a powerful sociological motivator. The notion of "keeping up with the Joneses" has been around for many generations. In pursuit of that goal, people who might otherwise be more inclined to be prudent and reserved might be prepared to throw caution to the wind and invest more heavily than before. When considering the real estate bubble, it should be obvious that many "investors" were merely scrambling to buy while mortgage rates were at generational lows.

TINA

Much like FOMO, the "there is no alternative" (TINA) ethos has its roots in social psychology. Rather than being driven by an implicit fear (falling behind because of not jumping onto the gravy train of a *bull market*), TINA is a form of greed that allows people to feel confident about stocks precisely because other options offer such lousy compensation in comparison. This could lead to high valuations and potentially to bubbles. People who have money to invest have to invest in something. Accordingly, even when stocks, bonds, and real estate are all near all-time highs, the money has to go somewhere. Governments know this. Rate hikes are rare in election years.

Resulting

The term *resulting* is one that you may not be familiar with. It refers to the tendency to judge a decision based on the outcome of that decision rather than the process and methods used to make the decision in the first place. Many people would say that buying a lottery ticket is a bad decision because lotteries are a "tax on the stupid," but if that lottery ticket comes up a winner, they might say that the decision to buy was a good one. How could a random outcome realized after the fact convert a previously bad decision into a good one? Changing the results causes people to change their assessment of a decision. The government ads in support of casinos and lotteries only show the outlier winners, not the army of losers. Accentuate the positive.

• • •

For better or worse, by the beginning of 2022, it seemed everyone had been doing whatever could be done to eliminate market downturns. If the results seemed favourable, the decisions seemed to be shrewd. Until rate hikes became unavoidable, no policymaker wanted to have the citizens experience a downturn on their watch. Instead of allowing for the traditional ebb and flow of market cyclicality, central bankers and finance ministers seemed determined to keep the good times rolling for as long as possible by using whatever means they had.

This is yet another unintended consequence of managing economies to function in perpetual growth mode. Virtually all central bankers are now talking about a slower growth rate such as has not been since the Great Depression of the 1930s. Politicians usually dodge and deflect when the subject comes up. The federal government issued economic updates that assured Canadians not to worry, even though the projected future deficits would climb even higher than previously imagined, depending on factors such as the severity of future shutdowns and the rate of Covid-19 infections. Out of curiosity, have you ever noticed how often governments portray certain spending initiatives as an "investment in our future" that will "pay dividends down the road"? The depiction may or may not be fair, but the public sector's co-opting of private sector lingo shows the eagerness to use a similar narrative.

Economic updates offered a vague commitment to spend between $70 billion and $100 billion over the ensuing years to restore the Canadian economy to its prepandemic employment levels. The justification for this proposed profligacy was that Canada had been put in the position of having a once-in-a-lifetime opportunity to "build back better," considering interest rates were at all-time lows. In fact, government went so far as to say that federal debt-servicing costs, relative to the size of Canada's economy, were at a hundred-year low. By late 2022, that rationale was no longer valid.

The post-pandemic spending target had a policy element to it, as well. The government would aim to manage GDP growth to a level above 3 percent. Until then, the government's immediate priority was to do "whatever it takes" to help Canadians and businesses stay safe and solvent. Once the storm had passed, the government would press on:

> We will ensure the Canadian economy that emerges from this pandemic is greener, more inclusive, more innovative, and more competitive than the one that preceded it, with a stronger, more resilient middle class ... We're going to roll those out when we roll out more details of our growth plan.

For context, the increased spending represented a big jump from the stimulus plan unveiled in response to the GFC. That response was valued at around 2.5 percent of GDP — roughly $47 billion over two years. It should be obvious that the minister's words offered a clear indication that this time the government was firmly committed to the continuance of economic growth at essentially all costs.

• • •

Facing the idea that economic growth should be pursued at all costs is the central challenge of our times. It is a challenge that is environmental, existential, and, most of all, behavioural. How can governments get people to get their heads around the sacrifices required because of the climate crisis when they simultaneously maintain a commitment to growth at all costs?

As of today, we have a government that is purportedly and simultaneously committed to strong GDP growth in the foreseeable future and to keeping our commitments to the 2015 Paris Accord on Climate Change as well. Until now, those two objectives were widely seen as mutually exclusive. Looked at from a more enlightened perspective, they may well be mutually supportive. What is required, it seems, is a narrative that allows those two seemingly disparate objectives to be reconciled in an actionable manner. Hey! Here's an idea: Why not spend money like mad to prop up the economy to prepare for the new world order where our hyper-reliance on burning hydrocarbons is reduced? It would allow us to shift our outlook from one of perpetual bullishness to one that envisions a world where growth is reduced and possibly even eliminated, but prosperity continues onward — albeit with somewhat different expectations.

One might note that we've heard this before. In late 2006, *The Economics of Climate Change: The Stern Review* was released by economist Nicholas Stern, chair of the Centre for Climate Change Economics and Policy at Leeds University and the London School of Economics. The report discussed the effect of global warming on the world economy and is likely still the most widely known and discussed report of its kind.

The review stated that climate change is the greatest and widest-ranging market failure ever seen, presenting a unique challenge for economics. It provided prescriptions, including environmental taxes to minimize the economic and social disruptions. The main conclusion was that the benefits of strong, early action on climate change far outweigh the costs of not acting and pointed to the potential impacts of climate change on water, resources, food, health, and the environment. Nearly twenty years after this urgent plea for action, little of substance has changed. As the saying goes, "When all is said and done, more will be said than done." The best opportunities for meaningful (i.e., relatively cheap) actions have already passed. Stern's main point, which has never been timelier, is that the longer we wait to fix our collective problem, the more it will cost.

We are now at a moment in history where the themes of market efficiency, risk management, and overly optimistic behavioural biases intersect. To that, we might add the concerns of properly incorporating externalities into market prices and properly calibrating our collective expectations of what the future might reasonably look like. How shall we proceed?

The political right has long exploited the collective *cognitive dissonance* that many voters face. These days, many resort to disinformation and denial to bolster that defence. People want a better future for their children, but they do not want to make sacrifices to their lifestyles presently. As a result, several false narratives have been allowed to take hold. There are plenty of people who are quite prepared to ignore things in the hope that they'll go away. For those who don't want to deal with the lifestyle choices that would be part of a meaningful response to the climate crisis, the easy "solution" is to deny the problem by calling it a hoax.

Citizens are not blameless. In fact, they are conspicuously culpable. The problem of Bullshift has been with us for decades already. We just choose not to confront it because it feels better to pretend everything's fine. Both as investors and as voters, we have been only too willing to buy into false narratives that make us feel good, rather than into true narratives that force us to confront difficult realities. This is entirely evident if we look south of the border. In the 2020 American presidential election, Donald Trump marshalled an astounding seventy-four million votes. This is clear proof that there are plenty of people who are willing to vote for what makes them feel good even if it means scientific evidence and plain truth must be parked at the door.

A significant part of the challenge revolves around dominant mindsets. Many people claim to take a long-term perspective. In reality, most elected politicians think in terms of four-year intervals, that being the time between most elections. People in finance tend to think a bit longer — perhaps one business cycle as compared to one electoral cycle. Business cycles typically last six to eight years. Notably, both sets of Bullshifters — financial advisers and politicians — would have us believe that a long-term perspective is less than a decade.

Doing irreparable harm to the planet has stunning implications for both economic growth and quality of life considerations. One would think that strategic, long-term thinkers would take the necessary steps to ensure long-term interests are being protected. Unfortunately, doing so requires that clients (be they voters or investors) are willing to make considerable sacrifices in the here and now. Alas, in the world of Bullshifters, there are virtually no sacrifices in the present — and only clear skies and happy

smiles in the future. For the better part of a generation, politicians who confronted climate change were routinely punished by voters, who would rather look the other way than make personal sacrifices. Climate change is the pre-eminent challenge of our generation; yet, to this day, there are entire political parties that cannot or will not even accept that climate change is real.

Many climate change deniers were elected again and again by constituents who were happy to vote based on self-serving careerism and community-based peer pressure rather than a dispassionate assessment of the evidence. Even while insisting they were forward-looking, long-term decision-makers, voters, and investors chose to look the other way rather than stare into the eyes of anything that required making sacrifices. Life is hard enough, according to these people, even though life has literally never been easier than for people in the Western world in the twenty-first century.

Denial not only fails to solve the problem; it allows people to divert their attention by not focusing enough on the very real and consequential challenges before us. The problem, of course, is that embracing an uncertain but presumptively green economic future requires that we let go of the current economic alignment. Even well-intended politicians who attempt to deal with the climate crisis are less than forthcoming about the challenges ahead. One of the new darling concepts of the 2020s is *modern monetary theory* (MMT), which suggests that as long as economic growth exceeds inflation, we'll be okay. There are two obvious challenges here. First, as we go to print, inflation is a massive problem, and no reasonable person would suggest sustainable growth is possible above the current inflation rate. Second, even if inflation were brought under control, economic growth is incompatible with environmental sustainability in the long term. The limits to growth, much like the endowments of planet earth, are finite.

The conclusion is that if we want to put an end to the Bullshift, we need to abandon thinking of MMT as a plausible way out. At best, MMT could be used to build critical green infrastructure in the short term to allow for a more purposeful transition. That transition, however, cannot come soon enough.

PART II

Since the Bullshift mindset of the finance industry has been reinforced with the Bullshift mindset of politicians who universally promise a better tomorrow, it is difficult for ordinary citizens to have a meaningful, adult conversation about how things will have to change to get from where we are now to where we need to be. That conversation is more necessary than ever.

Chapter 10

Guarding Against Bullshift

Understand bias to rethink your roles
It's up to you to champion your goals

IF YOU GENUINELY WANT TO BE "part of the solution," it is extremely difficult to acknowledge that, in a very real and tangible way, you are a significant part of the problem.

This is not the first time in history that an industry has had to confront its own demons. Big tobacco had its primary crisis of conscience in the 1960s and 1970s. That challenge has continued to this day, of course, but, along the way, the industry has changed because of new advertising regulations and required disclosures for public health impacts. Big oil had its first brush with the environmental reality caused by its products in the 1980s and its challenge of adaptation continues to the present, as well.

A quick refresher about Ignaz Semmelweis. Recall that people often reject new evidence that contradicts established beliefs, especially where self-interest and identity are involved. Semmelweis's best efforts to persuade his peers, even though he was armed with preliminary evidence that supported his views about the correlation between being sanitary and minimizing further harm, had no impact. He was unable to get the medical establishment to accept the correlation. After all, how could a doctor, who so earnestly wanted to save lives, be a primary contributor to unnecessary fatalities?

It is now considered possible that millions of people may have died unnecessarily because of the medical community's rejection of the Semmelweis thesis. What is self-evident today was considered heretical when first posited. For decades, physicians and surgeons simply refused to accept any responsibility for contributing to the problem. In fact, they were affronted by the thesis and turned Semmelweis into a pariah for having the audacity to suggest it.

We are now more attuned to how aspiring innovators need to overcome inherent bias against new ideas — or are we? Some of the current circumstances bring to mind the oil and tobacco companies of the past. Corporate interests have historically shown little interest in protecting the public from the negative effects of their products. As a result, governments have assumed a role in regulating them to protect the interests of the people. Unlike in the case of those industries, however, there is relatively little evidence that suggests a similar threat to the public interest can be attributed to the finance industry. So far. Mind you, no one is really looking for any threats, either. If it ain't broke, don't fix it. Then again, if "it" is broke, but no one knows, then it might be easiest to hide the evidence and keep it that way. Public ignorance is often a precondition of profit maximization.

If you think big tobacco and big oil have powerful lobbies, consider how powerful the lobbying efforts of big finance are. The financial services industry is far larger than the tobacco industry, notably larger than the energy industry, and widely considered to be the backbone of our economy. In the GFC, financial firms were deemed to be "too big to fail" and so were bailed out by governments that could not countenance the turmoil that could have ensued if the firms went under.

The industry may or may not have realized that by now; it is certain, though, that the general public has not. To date, there have been no equivalents to the U.S. surgeon general's report *Smoking and Health*, or the Nobel-winning Intergovernmental Panel on Climate Change, to act as catalysts.

We all remember the GFC that started in 2007 and ended in early 2009. Something similar started happening in 2020. It hasn't ended yet. This time, instead of bailing out billion-dollar corporations and providing liquidity to offset counterparty risks, our governments opted to prop up households by providing liquidity to them to offset the financial penalties imposed on them because of government-sanctioned job losses designed to protect public health. Income support programs and loan deferral initiatives were offered to help households get through the initial crisis. People were able to keep paying their debts, and by the end of the summer of 2020, we even saw household and consumer debt actually declining. This is cause for optimism.

By late 2020, Canada's minister of finance went so far as to call this support a "pre-loaded stimulus." We will need to keep a close eye on household debt levels, but the problem of their being crushing did not seem particularly imminent then. But by 2022, supply chain disruptions and a war in Europe caused inflation to climb to multi-generational highs and the optimistic storyline of public policy mavens engineering a soft landing became less and less credible.

The early 2020 response to the health crisis was both appropriate and necessary for the emergency we found ourselves in. Unfortunately, the solution to the health crisis was the catalyst for creating multi-asset class bubbles. This is like the GFC all over again. We're now dealing with the unintended consequences of well-intended public policy initiatives. We've solved one problem by creating another. The challenge may well be to get people to spend that preloaded stimulus that they'd rather bank. By the time Covid-19 began to subside in 2022, it was apparent that people might have to spend that stimulus money on higher debt payments.

What we as Canadians — and especially those of us in the financial services industry — need to recognize is that the hyperintense focus on keeping the economy moving at all costs has created a monster. Distorted price levels arising from the obsession with economic growth at all costs created market valuations that have reached obscene levels. Sometimes, solving one problem can leave you in a situation that is every bit as bad as the original.

There's an adage that lots of people want change; they just don't want to change. Understanding that things may need to be done differently in the future is something that many people can get behind. We simply need to lower our expectations about what the future might look like.

We'll need to divert money toward military expenditures to counteract thugs who happen to be leading countries. We'll need to divert government

Return experiences across generations

Annualized real returns on equities and bonds (%)

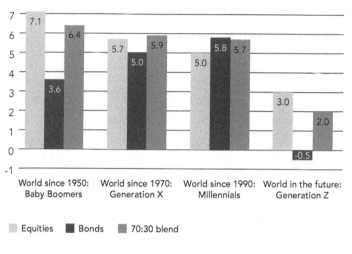

Source: Elroy Dimson, Paul Marsh, and Mike Staunton, *Global Investment Returns Yearbook 2021*, Credit Suisse, 2021.

Our children and grandchildren should expect returns far lower than anything we experienced. Who's going to tell them?

spending to pour hundreds of billions of dollars that might have otherwise been spent on traditional economic development into projects that reduce our carbon footprint. There will be refugees from war and refugees from climate and political unrest due to refugees all around.

Economic growth as we have known it in our lifetimes will not be seen again. People throughout the Western world need to come to terms with the lifestyle sacrifices necessary to transition to a sustainable economy. Obviously, if the economy is not growing, that means lower returns going forward. Politicians and advisers earn their keep by keeping their voters and clients happy with a positive view of the future. Alas, the truth hurts sometimes.

Asking those same people to make meaningful lifestyle sacrifices in the present is a different matter altogether. Canadian society in general, and particularly the financial services industry, needs to come to terms with the inconvenient truths of our time. One such truth is that markets work well when everything is incorporated into price, but poorly when a full-cost accounting is avoided.

Externalities, the Efficient Markets Hypothesis, and Carbon Taxes

This brings us to a point where three seemingly disparate considerations need to be contemplated simultaneously: *externalities*, the *efficient market hypothesis*, and carbon taxes. The first two are somewhat esoteric terms used by economists and finance experts. The third is a favourite of public policy geeks. Taken together, they point to how Bullshift has taken over the financial services mindset. Not everything has an explicit price, but most things that allow for unfettered competition are priced fairly. Those two thoughts need to be reconciled. Here are some simple working definitions for each term:

> ***Externality:*** A cost or benefit that is imposed by one or several parties on a third party who did not agree to incur that cost or be the recipient of that benefit.

> ***Efficient market hypothesis:*** The theory that stocks always trade at an approximately fair value, making it impossible for investors to reliably profit by purchasing undervalued stocks or selling stocks at inflated prices.

> **Carbon tax:** A tax on fossil fuel consumption, especially on fuel used by motor vehicles. It is intended to reduce the emission of carbon dioxide.

The interplay between these three things poses an intellectual threat to the financial services industry as we know it. An externality is something that is otherwise unaccounted for that offers a benefit for one party and creates a similar cost or costs for other parties as a result. One of the most common examples is pollution. Corporations that pollute without paying for the environmental harm they do get a free ride by making more money in part because the cost of pollution is not being absorbed by the polluter. The offending corporation gains in the form of higher profits; society loses in the form of a lower quality of life, higher health care costs, and the like.

Trading costs are an externality to portfolio performance just as pollution is an externality to industry. The remedy for high trading costs is to use low-cost products that track a benchmark efficiently. The remedy to the externality of pollution is to put a price on carbon emissions. Some politicians and some financial advisers who are happy with the status quo have no interest in actually solving the problem and might even go so far as to deny the problem exists. Unfortunately for them, carbon taxes and low-cost products like exchange-traded funds and index funds do exist. There is no reliable way to refute these solutions to the externality-based problems, so, rather than attacking the solution, some people choose to deny the problem.

Most people believe pollution should not be free. If there are no economic or societal consequences for polluting, corporations and individuals will feel free to pollute without fear of recrimination. Markets don't really take the pollution produced into account when putting a price on goods and services that are bought and sold. One might say that externalities represent a pricing inefficiency that can skew priorities to make less responsible companies look more profitable than they really are. It may be that addressing real and perceived market inefficiencies hasn't been a stated priority of government intervention for fear that doing so would have unintended consequences for the market.

For its part, the financial services industry has a self-interest in promoting the idea of market inefficiency. The irony is that much of the financial advice industry implies that markets *don't* work, because that stance is profitable for the industry. Denying market efficiency in finance is like denying climate change in the oil patch. The denial is rooted in *self-serving bias*, but, unlike with pollution, most advisers are not even remotely conscious of it.

OBJECTIVELY SPEAKING, THE FUTURE OF THE MARKETS
IS VERY VERY GOOD.

The debate about just how efficient markets are has raged for over half a century. Misinformation and misdirection are hallmarks of this "debate." The bullishness that the industry promotes is partly based on the idea that through hard work, shrewdness, and diligence, one might rationally expect to outperform the market. This is impossible in aggregate, but *motivated reasoning* is a powerful adversary, so impressionable investors often buy into it. Out of unconscious self-interest, some financial professionals want people to believe stock-picking works — and, due to greed and gullibility, investors want to believe their story.

The thing that the industry often fails to explain is that, since trading costs money, it is certain that, on average, a passive investor who buys products that track benchmarks will outperform an active investor who trades securities within those benchmarks, simply because the pre-cost performance of both groups is identical, but since the passive option costs less than the active option, the passive investor does better, on average.

Trading activity generates revenues for those doing the trading. The financial services industry has traditionally derived much of its revenue based on the premise that trading is likely to yield a profit. Is it any surprise that the industry would favour the inefficient viewpoint when the premise of inefficiency generates outsized income?

Please see the paper "The Arithmetic of Active Management" by Nobel laureate William F. Sharpe on my book website, standup.today, for more on the refutation of the idea that trading leads to market outperformance in aggregate. Markets work and are highly efficient if allowed to function properly. Accordingly, laissez-faire economic policies are seen by many as being the best and intervention is widely seen as being harmful. Externalities are a major reason for market mispricings and failures, because they don't allow the market to function properly. As such, policies that deal with externality mispricings have the opposite effect of traditional interventions. Traditional interventions get in the way and distort markets.

Further evidence shows that most actively managed mutual funds consistently underperform their benchmarks over all timeframes and in all geographical jurisdictions. This should come as no surprise. The opposite would be an example of the so-called *Lake Wobegon effect*, where nearly everyone is above average.

Carbon taxes have been discussed in economic circles for many decades now. No one really doubts that they would alter consumption patterns if implemented at meaningful levels. Many people hate them because they feel the state is forcing them to make decisions that they might not otherwise make. Note how self-interest plays a role. Have you ever noticed that it is only smokers who are opposed to the punitive taxes levied on cigarettes? Non-smokers almost never give it a moment's thought. People respond to incentives — and disincentives. People don't like to have their behaviour manipulated — unless, of course, they think that manipulation will leave them better off.

The thing about carbon taxes is that they can convert markets that have significant externalities — and are inefficiently priced as a result — into markets that are fairly priced through the proper incorporation of those externality mispricings into the ultimate pricing. Efficiency is good. It allows prices to be set fairly for everyone. One might ask whether the failure to incorporate externalities into market pricing is an inefficiency or a behavioural bias. They are not necessarily mutually exclusive. It may well be that the failure to incorporate externalities into prices is an example of both.

As a society, we have grown coddled and entitled. The sacrifices required to move forward with confidence are tiny in comparison to those made by previous generations. Despite this, it seems people throughout the Western world — people who are both investors and voters — are unwilling to make the necessary changes. We are not unable. The wherewithal is there. We simply lack the will to make the necessary changes and will choose to deny reality to continue going about our comfortable lives with as few disruptions as possible. Big finance and big oil have much in common. Because the environmental threat is existential in nature, the threat from finance industry Bullshift seems to go largely ignored.

In 2006, U.S. president George W. Bush admitted that the United States was addicted to oil. A grudging, but self-evident acknowledgement. Today, we need politicians to come clean and admit that all Western economies are addicted to something related, but different — economic growth — especially to the kind that comes at any cost. As with any addiction, withdrawal can lead to some frightening circumstances and side effects. It might be better to wean ourselves off the dependency a little more slowly. In the recent past, virtually every element of economic policy in the West has been predicated on continued economic expansion.

In October 2008, federal Liberal leader Stéphane Dion campaigned on the idea of a "Green Shift" by offering to introduce a carbon tax and offset it through a reduction in income tax. The idea was to make it revenue neutral. Voters hated it. Dion was directionally right in his thinking, of course, but people weren't ready. The opposite of inconvenient truths is convenient lies. That's what voters chose in 2008. The idea of replacing a longstanding income tax with a new, targeted consumption tax was a political non-starter.

Cognitive dissonance and *motivated reasoning* were at it again — this time on the part of voters. Much like the people who voted for Donald Trump in 2016 and 2020, people believed what they wanted to believe, facts be damned. It seems a philosophical choice is required. When externalities that do not incorporate important considerations persist, this can lead to markets being inefficient to the point of being wildly distorted. What to do? Left with the choice between intervention (i.e., implementing a carbon tax to offset a mispricing anomaly) and allowing imperfect markets to function as they have always done while pretending that everything is fine (i.e., not implementing a tax), right-leaning governments have opted for the latter. The explanation is simple. Evidence shows that people are simply lousy at quantifying and calibrating big, non-obvious, long-term externalities into their thinking. One might call it *recency bias* or *status quo bias*, but whatever the case, we predictably choose options that maintain current lifestyles while minimizing change in preestablished behaviour.

Without externalities you can't take the position that markets are inherently efficient and then espouse carbon taxes. One of the goals of carbon taxes is to readjust pricing to account for the mispricings caused by externalities that were unaccounted for previously. In for a penny, in for a pound. Once one buys into the inefficiency ethos, one must apply it across the board, if only for the sake of consistency. Carbon taxes are needed precisely because markets work. If implemented at a fair level, they would ensure the fair and efficient functioning of capital markets by putting a price on externalities where no such price existed previously.

The persistent notion of market inefficiency is hard to shake and has held sway in the industry since its inception. It's seen as "good for business" because it allows advisers to charge for services that presumptively add value. Since the evidence shows beyond any doubt that there is, in fact, no added value in trading stocks in aggregate, the ruse of ongoing inefficiency must be maintained despite overwhelming evidence to the contrary. This is done to keep the money flowing.

It seems likely that many advisers suffer from a corollary of the *Lake Wobegon effect*: the natural human tendency to overestimate one's capabilities in relation to others. In fairness, the affliction is not the exclusive domain of people working in the financial services industry. The effect has been observed among drivers, CEOs, stock market analysts, college students, and many others.

Low Rates as the Pretense for Green Infrastructure

The seeds of the immediate policy solution to the pandemic sprouted and grew into something distinct, separate, and insidious. The "solution" created a massive multi-asset bubble based on cheap money and easy credit. The problem was exacerbated by consumers flush with overconfidence, *recency bias*, and the complete lack of viable investment alternatives. It seemed no one cared about *loss aversion* or *prospect theory* whatsoever. Unwittingly, much as in the GFC of 2007 to 2009, government created a massive market bubble as a direct result of well-intended, but misguided, policies.

The bubbles that were manufactured by public policy initiatives grew to be so huge precisely because they were supported by the financial services industry. The unhealthy "we've got your back" rhetoric came into play early in the pandemic, with the federal government reaching out to people about mortgage deferrals, income supports, and the like. It shows the seamless coordination of finance and government efforts to communicate a reassuring and confidence-building message. It was the right thing to do at the time, but a monster was unwittingly being created.

The Chinese word for crisis is frequently but somewhat incorrectly said to be composed of two Chinese characters signifying "danger" and "opportunity." There can be little doubt that 2020 was the virtual embodiment of the word *crisis*. Generational highs for market valuations represented an obvious danger, but what, exactly, was the opportunity?

Throughout history, politicians have used events as justifications for pursuing courses of action for which they had no clear mandate when elected to office. Rather, an opportunity came along after they were installed — events could be used to construct a plausible storyline that justified doing things that the government would have preferred to do but, in the absence of those events, might not have been as easy to justify. Fortune favours the prepared, and all-time-low interest rates provided politicians of all stripes with an opportunity to spend like never before on whatever they felt was important. The cost to service the multi-generational debt levels being incurred was now — and would certainly continue to be — at rock bottom.

After the Stern report was released in 2006, economists had been insisting that significant action was needed on climate change. From the perspective of simple costs and benefits, there was a clear need to act urgently, too. Dion tried to capture the public consciousness around the time the report was released but failed miserably. In 2020 it looked like we would have a chance to get things right. Justin Trudeau, a young and charismatic prime minister, seemed more like what one might expect as a leader who prioritizes the environment. Canada was going to try again to effect real change. Low interest rates provided the intellectual cover to proceed with confidence. Given the current economic circumstances and a recent history of dithering by both Liberal and Conservative governments, an activist agenda seemed to make sense. Time was of the essence. Trudeau saw his moment and seized it.

The autumn of 2020 saw the presentation of a throne speech, the release of an economic update, a change in finance minister, and a change in deputy finance minister — all in just over two months. In keeping with ideas that had been bandied about at the World Economic Forum in Davos earlier that year, the government would embark on a "Great Reset" to, among other priorities, comply with obligations made in the Paris Accord in 2015. Some have taken to calling this a "Green New Deal." Whatever the preferred terminology, a policy shift of epic proportions seemed to be in the offing. A policy initiative that was once referred to as a "Green Shift" was about to collide head-on with the systemic biases of financial services industry Bullshift. How would they be reconciled?

At first glance, financial services Bullshift and a government-sponsored Green Shift seem like opposites. They are not. In fact, they are, for the short term at least, mutually supportive. Bullshift is about perpetual growth and optimism. Any meaningful reset deals with the imperative of building transit and other infrastructure, retrofitting houses and offices, and moving to clean energy. That means economic activity that is made possible through public expenditures on big-money projects. Jobs galore. A booming economy.

If the stock market were to take a serious tumble, such a program would be welcomed as being introduced at an ideal time for high-level public sector expenditure and job creation. The private sector would be reeling, and the government would be in a unique position to create jobs, backstop business-es financially, and finally keep promises that had been made but not acted on for many years. The federal government committed to massive spending over the years starting in 2021, when everything was otherwise getting back to normal.

Also, in late 2020, the federal government announced that it would finally be proceeding with increases in the federal carbon tax to comply with Paris targets. By early 2021, the Supreme Court of Canada ruled that the federal government had the constitutional right to impose a national carbon tax. Given the division of powers in Canada, it might not have been possible to do much more than what was done. Rebate cheques would move from being distributed annually to being distributed quarterly to keep the initiative top of mind and to generate some positive buzz. Finally, belatedly, a meaningful environmental policy predicated on an enforceable federal carbon tax was coming into focus.

Change Is Upon Us

The economy is going to go into transition. It must. The years from around 2022 to 2030 may well be punctuated by massive government spending to create jobs and fast-track a transition to a green economy. The primary policy aim is and has always been long-term prosperity. The challenge, how-ever, is one of achieving that prosperity without growth as we have come to know it.

Returning briefly to former Bank of Canada governor Stephen Poloz and his five "tectonic forces," we can begin to see what's likely on the horizon. He suggested that these five trends would combine to create unpredictable outcomes, but that risk management is still a core need. One of the specific prescriptions Poloz put forward involved the need to promote deliberately inflationary policies in the short term to counteract systemic deflationary trends. Here's where he revealed his *modern monetary theory* bias: he was emphatic that headline growth would have to exceed interest rates and that rates, in turn, would need to normalize around a level something like 2 percent. Basically, he said we would need to grow our way out of the problem. Noting that the national debt to GDP ratio was like what was experienced in the aftermath of the Second World War, he did not see this as an insurmountable challenge.

Still, for this approach to succeed, we would need for GDP to grow at a rate of 3 percent or higher — with inflation settling under 3 percent. Given how anemic economic growth had been even before the pandemic hit, and how high and persistent inflation seems to be as we go to press, that's a tall order.

Canada has been experiencing a so-called K-shaped recovery, where many industries rebounded quickly and resumed an upward trajectory once the original crisis was brought under control, but other lines of business, including restaurants, cinemas, travel companies, and hotels, to name a few, were looking at the stark possibility of being forever changed by the new world order. What's needed is a recovery that is not only strong but also fairly evenly distributed.

• • •

Whether in terms of investment opportunities or broad, international economic trends, it seems as though the good times are in the past for the Western economies. For decades now, the West has been stagnant in terms of quality of life, life expectancy, real wages, and the like. Meanwhile, the developing world has been closing the gap on these and many other metrics.

The Milton Friedman concept of trickledown economics, which features tax cuts for the wealthy, is widely seen to have failed to produce the sustainable growth it promised. Worse still, that approach is now also seen as having exacerbated the modern-day problem of inequality. A couple of generations ago, societal happiness and an improved quality of life were natural extensions of a large and growing economy. Today, that paradigm is coming under increasing pressure. The dismissive rhetorical question, "Have you been trickled on lately?" is used by those with low and middle incomes to underscore that the well-intended ideas of the past have been repudiated by a generation whose personal experiences have fallen far short of what was promised to them.

The *Gini coefficient*, which has given way to the *Gini index*, is named after Corrado Gini. It measures the distribution of income across the broad population. In many nations that embraced Friedman's views, the index has been trending higher — meaning inequality is increasing. More contemporary environmental economists like Tim Jackson have noticed this growing gap in income and posited that it was inevitable. Full-cost-accounting economists take externalities into consideration and self-evidently point out that since economic growth cannot continue indefinitely, GDP growth should be abandoned as the dominant way of keeping score. To hear them tell it, GDP growth has always been a poor benchmark for economic progress because it is unsustainable.

Another age-old economic concept is that of *Pareto optimality*. Vilfredo Pareto pioneered the concept of looking for solutions that make as many people better off as possible, while simultaneously doing no harm. This is an idea that many people believe has an intuitive charm. Friedman's disciples routinely reject it. Taken together, these two concepts, both pioneered by Italian economists, are likely the economic models most often associated with the issue of income disparity. Having been mostly dismissed in the past few decades, both are making a comeback of sorts. Trickledown economics created a societal monster where plutocrats have enormous power and influence, both of which come at the expense of virtually everyone else. Naturally, and with a handful of high-profile but notable exceptions, the 0.1 percent at the top of the income food chain will advocate for policies that protect their interests. Until very recently, these interests have not included a full consideration of environmental, social, or governance (ESG) factors. That is beginning to change.

Somewhere along the way, the financial services industry became the biggest cheerleader for monetarism and trickledown thinking. Financial advisers love the likes of Friedman but are less likely to embrace the likes of Gini and Pareto. Bullshift requires an adherence to the view that optimism, growth, and a shiny new tomorrow are just around the corner for all of us.

Many advisers are ambivalent toward the behavioural economists referenced here and are unwilling to incorporate the teachings of *behavioural economics* into the advice they give. *Behavioural economics* has not yet made the journey from academic textbooks to adviser playbooks.

Don't Worry, Be Happy

The Bobby McFerrin song and ethos of "Don't Worry, Be Happy" fit the financial services industry of the past, but the industry is now in a new reality that is far less rosy. There is little doubt that governments can and will do whatever it takes to keep the economy moving forward, but governments can only do so much and for so long. One day soon we will wake up and find that the economic growth that we have all come to expect throughout our entire lives will no longer exist as an innate characteristic of our environment. Worse still, it will be obvious that there will be no available public policy levers to manufacture a stable and accretive growth rate, either. When economic growth grinds to something like a halt, what happens next?

It should be obvious that the first thing we will need to adjust are our return expectations — downward. Investment returns are going to be much, much lower. Probably even shockingly lower. As a result, this might be a good time to revisit the exercise from chapter 5. That case study used the return assumptions as set out by FP Canada. Many people are of the opinion that the FP Canada Assumptions Guidelines are embarrassingly high — still. To me, a more appropriate framework for long-term return assumptions could be calculated quickly and easily using readily available information and modified modestly using historical sensitivities. The parameters are as follows:

o   Use the current ten-year, twenty-year, and thirty-year bond yields to estimate rates over those timeframes.

o   Adopt the widely accepted view that the historical risk premium of stocks over bonds is up to 5 percent, annualized.

o   Modify the spread between the two numbers above using the CAPE for the market in question and modify the return expectation up or down by the deviation from the long-term average.

No More Great Expectations

Everyone needs to reset their thinking. The great reset is not only a public policy admonition; it is a public consciousness imperative. Have you ever met any advisers who refer to themselves as "cautiously pessimistic"? Or a stock picker who tells you we are NOT in a stock picker's market? Or a stock picker who admits to being below average? Didn't think so. We all need to lower our expectations regarding future returns and how we'll perform compared to others.

The realization that, in terms of economic growth and prosperity at least, things will not get better needs to make its way into the public consciousness. Since every generation has grown up expecting things to be better for themselves than for their parents — and better for their children than for themselves — you can see how societal *cognitive dissonance* is a massive attitudinal challenge.

Don't wait for the politicians to tell you, either. By its very nature, politics is the only industry that is even more dependent on Bullshift than is finance. Since the beginning of democracy, the main promises have been along the lines of a chicken in every pot and a car in every driveway. Our expectations about the future — both economic and environmental (as if they were different things) — are obviously calibrated incorrectly. They are far too high. Failure to recalibrate is reckless. The societal complacency about the good times lasting indefinitely is astonishing.

Specifically, the world has still not come to terms with the sacrifices that will be necessary. If we are being honest about what is required to get to a 40 percent greenhouse gas emissions target by 2035 and to net zero by 2050, we will have to acknowledge that we can only reach those targets if we accept significant reductions in both lifestyle and prosperity.

Some advisers have done a remarkably good job at getting the public to buy into their Bullshift. As colleagues of mine like to say, "the bears never

seem to gather any assets." Now, we can quibble about the distinction between a stock market bear and a capital market realist, but the point remains
valid. We all need to come clean and change the way we keep score. Most of
all, we need the public to buy in to the gravity of the challenge. The problem
is that we, as a society, have become preconditioned to expect "progress" in
its various forms and cannot abide being told that the metrics of the past
either will not apply or will not be as positive as we have come to expect.
Some advisers seem biased, unwittingly, to be all positive, all the time. Most
of the time and for most people in the past, that attitudinal pre-set is harm-
less and perhaps even helpful. Just because this is usually so doesn't mean it
is necessarily so. Unfortunately, because the history of the Western world in
the post–Second World War era has been one of inexorable and remarkable
progress, voters and investors in the Western world see economic and lifestyle progress as a birthright.

The good news, since some advisers are so very optimistic, is that while
things likely won't get better in the way we've come to expect, they don't
necessarily have to get worse, either. Because we have all experienced many
generations of measurable quality of life improvements, flatlining will feel
like a step backward to many. Some qualitative improvements cannot be
reliably measured, but are real, nonetheless. Fewer commutes. Quality time
with family. Cleaner air. Better health. Those sorts of things are often referred to as "priceless." In this instance, the word *priceless* is literal. Too often
in the past, economists have kept score based on tangible, measurable things
like GDP, household income, and trade balances. Not everything that can
be measured should be measured, however.

Our federal politicians are turning the corner on this challenge in a
favourable but remarkably sneaky way. Since buy-in from the public is both
necessary and difficult, I approve of their gambit. It goes something like this:

o people vote for politicians who spout Bullshift; and
o plainly telling the truth is often bad for your electoral pros-
   pects; but
o if you tell the truth in a way that sounds like Bullshift, you
   might just be able to get re-elected.

It is generally accepted that there are two primary levers to provide fiscal stimulus: tax less or spend more. Governments (plural, because it seems to be true of all levels and all jurisdictions) have chosen the latter. Tax increases are political suicide. Tax cuts are similar, because you must either lose the revenue stream forever or you must put taxes back to where they used to be — if you don't, a suicidal tax hike will be required eventually — so politicians have chosen not to pursue that route. Besides, if you can get people to keep their jobs and their homes, they'll be back in business as reliable taxpayers in no time. In theory, at least. Furthermore, since governments can borrow at far more favourable rates than households, it's just common sense to put the tab on the government's line of credit rather than on the citizens' credit cards.

Federally, a quick hat tip to the recent popularity of green bonds may be useful. It's one way governments can have their cake and eat it too — by increasing debt levels (presumptively bad) to fund sustainable growth and infrastructure projects (presumptively good). Governments love touting the high demand for green bonds and their oversubscription. The thinking is that when government spending stops and consumer demand stabilizes, tax revenues will return.

Many fear that a significant recession started in 2020 and that a larger crisis was averted through purposeful public policy. Perhaps "delayed" is a better word. As of 2022, a *bear market* may be upon us. If that happens, many will suggest that the so-called normalization of circumstances would explain it. Things were dicey in early 2020 and went south quickly when the pandemic hit. Then, things got better for the next year and three quarters, because of a massive series of interventions that worked better than anyone could have imagined. Finally, when the interventions stopped, the drawdown that started in 2020 resumed as though the pandemic experience had been a dream. People woke up to the reality that the economy and capital markets were indeed fragile all along and that they only appeared to be flourishing, because they were being artificially propped up.

The initial response was entirely proper and should be commended. The challenge now is, since consumption drives growth, how can we incentivize people to spend all that money they've been given? And how can we do it in a way that is environmentally sustainable? Increasing consumption in challenging economic times is hard enough. Doing so in a way that reduces our carbon footprint is harder still. It seems the only way to turn the corner is for governments to actively spend whatever money they have discretion over on long-term sustainability projects that have a positive net payoff over time.

For politicians, if the move is framed in terms of "preloaded stimulus," or "transitioning to a green economy," or "building back better," then maybe, just maybe, voters will be on board with it. What is required above all else is the notion that GDP growth can be maintained at a level at or above the level of inflation to present a plausible way out of an enormous ocean of public debt.

For advisers, if the move is framed as justification for moving to ESG methodologies, celebrating how capitalism has lifted literally billions of the developing world's inhabitants out of poverty and created a genuinely better future for everyone, then they will have found a channel for their optimism. Moving toward a greener future is an imperative that cannot be overstated. Anyone who claims to take a long-term perspective would need to concede that there is no longer timeframe than the rest of eternity. What's at stake now involves that kind of timeframe. If successful, they will have acted in a way that offers honour and integrity. There is no doubt in my mind that financial advisers will ultimately be part of the solution. Since we are all inhabitants of planet earth, this is almost certainly the purest form of stakeholder capitalism.

For investors, managing costs will become more important than ever in a low-return environment. In addition to being conscious of Bullshift, people would do well to incorporate a "full thrift" mindset. More than ever, we'll need to live within our means. Give your business to advisers who resist using Bullshift. Give your votes to politicians who resist using Bullshift, too. Focus on evidence. Don't make biased decisions based on emotion. Practice decision hygiene by thinking slowly and critically.

For consumers (i.e., for everyone), there will be an uncommon and unprecedented imperative to continue spending in tough times. That's counterintuitive, but likely necessary. The way forward may well involve threading a needle between spending enough on processes and technologies that are accretive to the planet without running our economy into the ground.

We need to move to a more sustainable economic model because the goal of perpetual growth is simply unrealistic. More like impossible. Until now, however, it has been all too easy for corporate and political interests wedded to Bullshift to convince the public that, as an example, it was a "good idea" that we should allow people and businesses to pollute for free. It was never a good idea, and the refusal to acknowledge externalities went on for far too long. We will all need to make lifestyle sacrifices in the future. This may well include increasing your savings rate, because the growth of capital markets may not be able to do the heavy lifting that it has done in the past. The can was kicked down the road for over a generation.

People Are Oblivious to Their Own Biases

Some financial advisers have become a lot like some right-leaning politicians. Many seem inclined toward viewing evidence through the lenses of *motivated reasoning* and *overconfidence*. That biased reasoning ethos runs deep, precisely because it strikes at the heart of adviser identity. Financial advisers sincerely want to be helpful and unbiased and firmly believe that they are helpful and unbiased. Nonetheless, the predisposition toward optimism can cloud judgment and cause people to miss opportunities and risks because of the blind spots harboured by that optimism.

However, some of us don't stop to ask why we believe what we believe. When the facts are bad for our business or for our reputation, the response from many of us is to deny them. The financial services industry of today has a lot in common with big oil and big tobacco of decades past. At least those industries were aware of their self-serving denials. Much of the financial services industry remains blissfully unaware of its own bias.

A necessary precondition of solving a problem is acknowledging that the problem exists in the first place. That's why Alcoholics Anonymous meetings begin with the frank statement that "My name is X, and I'm an alcoholic." Daniel Kahneman absolutely insists that everyone has some degree of bias in them. Given that, saying financial advisers are biased is not so much an indictment as it is a recognition of their humanity. Still, a little humility would likely do everyone some good. Maybe self-help groups could be set up. Imagine if at your first meeting with a new adviser the adviser said something like, "My name is Fred, and I have biases that creep into the advice I provide."

For decades, the financial services industry has been built on the premise that advisers add value because of the services they offer, which is possible because of the expertise they have. Efficient markets render traditional stock picking, decisions about market timing, sector rotation, seasonality, and various other approaches all but useless. Financial advisers around the world have come to be at least dismissive of, and often openly hostile to, evidence that threatens their narrative of adding value through behaviour modification. That's especially ironic given that evidence seems to suggest it's adviser behaviour that most needs to be modified.

Professor Sunita Sah of Cornell University argues that we are more likely to see real progress if we can identify and change the professional norms that influence behaviour. The problem is not one of virtue — or the lack thereof — so much as it is one of self-awareness — or the lack thereof.

In other words, professionals are much more prone toward a lazy conformity than they are to ethics-compromising practices. It's subtle. It's pervasive. And it happens all the time and to everybody. That's what happened with Arthur Andersen and Enron. That's what happened with the bond rating agencies leading to the GFC. Companies and individuals can lose their moral compasses if they are not vigilant in guarding against unwitting backsliding. Financial advisers are just like other actors in the professions. They have blithely and unwittingly gone about their business without a true contemplation of much of the evidence that questions their utility. Why would anyone bother to check their own behaviour when their motives are pure?

Are There Any Solutions?

As we have seen, it is much easier to make money by exploiting people's irrationality than it is to correct that irrationality. People will cling to their "right to be wrong" if it can make them feel good. *Cognitive dissonance* makes combating biases a challenge unlike any other because it involves solving a problem that people don't want to admit even exists. Humans have a long history of doing what they want to do to get what they want to get.

Social media not only compromise independent and critical thought, they create echo chambers where participants listen almost exclusively to like-minded people, thereby over-estimating both the popularity and the righteousness of whatever viewpoint they espouse. Perhaps most alarmingly, people increasingly look for social proof rather than empirical proof.

The simple fact is that the world has changed, and you need to know how to deal with it. Here's what I recommend:

o   Seek truth in all things.
o   Do not delude yourself into thinking the economic growth that has been fuelled by depleting harmful and non-renewable resources can go on indefinitely.
o   Ask your adviser about *optimism bias* as a general source of concern.

Ask your adviser if they have ever considered their own potential for bias and what might be done to manage it. Then, while you're at it, ask yourself the same question. For all the necessary introspection, listen to the answer carefully. Try to understand, not to judge.

The case studies offer examples of where attitudes and assumptions could be reconsidered. Consider what could go wrong and for how long when managing your portfolio. When preparing a financial plan, insist on using reasonable assumptions, because the return expectations you're using now are almost certain to be too high and costs need to be incorporated into the projection.

Furthermore, life expectancy may well be longer than you think and the risk of running out of money may well increase, so consider taking CPP as late as is practical — likely at age seventy.

o   Ask your adviser about the extent to which ESG products might be incorporated into your portfolio.

o Give serious consideration to increasing your exposure to emerging-market equities, because emerging-market economies are the fastest-growing part of the world.

o While you're at it, give serious consideration to increasing your exposure to alternative assets and tangibles.

o Be cautiously optimistic, but doggedly realistic as your default attitude to life.

No one has ever solved a problem that that person could not even identify in the first place. *Optimism bias* in the financial advice business has always been a factor, but it is only now becoming a source of concern. That optimism has had a mostly positive impact on people's lives, livelihoods, and portfolios ... until now. Going forward, however, jaunty optimism could provide us all with a Darwinian natural-selection sorting of mindsets. The past is not necessarily prologue. The future may not be as bright as we expected it to be, but it doesn't have to be bleak, either. Can you adapt to the new reality, which is really the same reality as it always was, just reconsidered in more realistic terms?

Take off the rose-coloured glasses. See the world as it really is. Become resigned to the prospect of more risk yielding lower return. Be prepared to work longer and to live longer. Lower your expectations. Stop what you're doing long enough to think critically and consider options purposefully.

• • •

If you want to learn more about transparency and integrity in the financial services industry, visit my website at standup.today. My advisory site is standupadvisors.ca.

Afterword

What Can Be Done About Bullshift?

IT'S FINE AND WELL TO IDENTIFY PROBLEMS, but the rubber hits the road when the discussion turns to solutions. Remember the context — unconscious bias is everywhere, and everyone, including those with the best intentions, has it. We live in a world where political leaders try to keep voters happy through policy intervention that involves minimal lifestyle sacrifice. While they say we can "grow our way out of the problem," current events like war and supply-chain disruptions, and ongoing demographic trends like low fertility and an aging workforce, make this rather unlikely. In fact, we will likely see slower growth and higher inflation.

Finding solutions to these problems is especially daunting because people are hard-wired to seek short-term gratification. They don't properly discount negative things, because it's easier to deny them. As a result, long-term and slow-moving macro trends like climate change are not scrutinized in a way that leads to rational decision-making. A full-cost accounting that includes the environmental impact of climate change is a concept few money managers appreciate. This is ironic, because the financial services community always tells us to think long-term.

Bertrand Russell said, "In the modern world, the stupid are cocksure while the intelligent are full of doubt." I agree, but the problem is even worse. Not only are the stupid cocksure, but so are ordinary people who let their optimism compromise their thinking. The challenge is to find specific, tangible interventions that work.

Everyone wants to be happy. The American Constitution even declares that citizens are entitled to "the pursuit of happiness." Political leaders speak of happiness as a basic human right; the hard truth is they have no idea how to achieve it for the people whose votes they seek. Ironically, those political leaders representing parties not in government take the opposing view. To them, everything is awful. Reality usually rests somewhere between the two extremes.

The Western world has what's known as a *base effect problem*, which distorts expectations of the future. With few exceptions, we are accustomed to strong economic growth and steady market increases. Neither is likely in the future. People in the developed world feel entitled and think because things always got better in the past, the trend will continue. We can't deny that the attitude exists. No one wants to be Chicken Little; no one wants to tell everyone the sky is falling — and absolutely no one wants to hear that message.

The simple solution to *optimism bias* is to park your predispositions at the door. Easier said than done. For three-quarters of a century, times were good, the economy grew, and optimism got rewarded. We now need to recognize that our lives and the lives of our parents were anomalies and that we should temper our optimism accordingly. Our children will not have the luxury to just assume that there will always be economic progress. We need to recognize this, and we need to figure out what to do with that knowledge. Evidence shows that optimistic people are happier and more inclined to take outsized risks. This means happiness sometimes leads to recklessness. It's like an addictive drug. Even if you recognize your addiction, you still need to find a way to overcome it, and you need the willpower to follow through on that strategy. As a society, we seem to lack both the self-awareness needed at this stage of our existence and the will to see things through.

Like many things in life, the solution is in how we choose to direct our attention. Yoga, meditation, and mindfulness would likely help overcome Bullshift. People can be happy without being overly optimistic, but they need to change how they keep score. Perhaps we could aim for mere contentment and wanting only what we already have. That would mean thinking more about future generations than we do about ourselves. No one is suggesting that people should aim to be unhappy or less happy. Just be more self-aware.

There are a few ways we can make a more conscious effort to be more self-aware, but one of the more obvious ones revolves around our mundane lives. Social media are a double-edged sword that help us feel connected, but promote thinking like the masses, and they are the home of countless trolls that suck the happiness right out of you. Since not everyone likes you it's best not to take everything personally. Exercise the right to think for yourself, but be accountable for what you say and do.

Now let's move on from passive attitudes to active thinking and real behaviour change. Consider the following:

o Actively seek out alternative views.
o Identify your own biases.
o Move from thinking fast to thinking slow.
o Consider what might go wrong, including the worst possible outcome.
o Learn the difference between following a narrative and analyzing facts. Put another way, be more rational and less emotional.

We would do well to recognize that the financial services industry has unwittingly engaged in a form of optimistic manipulation. Optimism has a place in the financial services industry, and for generations it has been a force for good. One consultant I know says that people who hire advisers are three times happier than those who don't, and they experience gratefulness, impact, intent, and fulfillment. The fact is, advisers acquire clients by making them feel good about themselves, not by disturbing them about tightening their belts.

I have a colleague who says it's more fun being an optimist and that advisers get paid for being that way. I disagree with the second part. Advisers get paid for offering measured advice customized to their clients' unique circumstances. Advisers dealing with high-net-worth clients since the end of the Second World War have been rewarded handsomely for being optimistic. Until now. Today's world is different, and we'd better recognize it. If we don't, optimism may for the first time in our lives prove very harmful.

• • •

Bookshelves are filled with feel-good, self-help prescriptions extolling the you-can-do-it mindset; this book challenges that mindset. Like most of you, I consider myself an optimist. But writing and researching this book has forced me to reflect on my own attitudes — what they are and where they come from. My hope is that readers will reflect on the biases they have and take the necessary steps to ensure the best possible outcome.

Acknowledgements

THERE'S AN OLD QUIP ORIGINALLY attributed to Billy Noonan: "If I had known I was going to live so long, I'd have taken better care of myself." For my part, if I had known this project was going to go on so long, I probably wouldn't have even started. Writing *Bullshift* has been a labour of love simply because there was a constant stream of new ideas that sprung from what was originally a simple, single idea about dealing with a pandemic. The first acknowledgement, therefore, is to Covid-19. Were it not for being sent home for an indefinite period on March 13, 2020, I almost certainly would not have even started writing.

Some people just know they were born to be writers. Not me. Over the years, I have learned that there are things that annoy me a lot that most others don't even care about. Writing about my concerns is the only way I can "let things go" when they start getting on my nerves. I feel like I'm constantly prepping for some future debate with some undefined opponent who simply doesn't see things my way — possibly because that person has not stopped to think about what is bugging me in the first place. Writing is a cathartic release that allows me to memorialize my frustrations so that I can move on. I started writing because I felt I "had to" more than out of any burning desire to do so.

The original draft of the manuscript was more or less done by the end of 2020, but my friend Kelley Keehn told me that if I wanted to get serious exposure for my ideas, I'd need to sign on with a major publisher, and in order to do that, I needed an agent. I started working with Jerry Amernic in the spring of 2021, and it was Jerry who got me to be more focused and verbally parsimonious in my writing. Jerry made me better and started the process of introducing me to media figures so that I could share my thesis that people unwittingly take on more risk than they think.

Jerry introduced me to Bill Hanna, who signed on as my agent in the summer of 2021. *Bullshift* is my third book, but both *The Professional Financial Adviser* and *STANDUP to the Financial Services Industry* were essentially self-published, so I knew that getting it published was going to be a bigger challenge. Bill was determined to help a principled portfolio manager step away from his day job long enough to score a gig with a major publisher in order to bring some important concerns to the surface. By the end of the year, Bill had worked his magic and negotiated a contract with Kathryn Lane of Dundurn Press. I was delighted!

In early 2022, the contract with Dundurn was officially signed and the tough slog of converting a rambling year-old manuscript into a coherent, updated, and readable book began in earnest. By that time, I was also making regular contributions to the *Financial Post* Friday newsletter, thanks to the support of Julie Cazzin, and to the *Globe and Mail*, courtesy of James Cowan. My challenge in writing for the national press was to provide meaningful commentary about investing, planning, and current events without cannibalizing the material in my book.

In addition to associate publisher Kathryn Lane, managing editor Elena Radic helped keep the project going. We tweaked the subtitle four times, I think. Publicist Alyssa Boyden worked out marketing blurbs and got overseas representatives to offer their thoughts on promotion, while designer Karen Alexiou completed the cover design and book interior. This was all done in the first half of 2022 while the edits were being completed. It was seamless. It was also fun to spend time thinking about how much better it was to have a support team helping to bring *Bullshift* to the public.

The heavy lifting was done by my editor, Dominic Farrell. No amount of Strunk and White preparatory reading can prepare a part-time writer for the rigours of working with a professional editor. Dominic was always helpful and candid. There is a natural tendency shared by almost all writers to want to keep as much of the original content as possible in the final version of the manuscript — after all, it was hard work to craft it in the first place. More than anyone else, Dominic convinced me that "less is more" and that chopping the word count by 5 percent would make for a more readable text, one that presents my thoughts in a clear way and avoids inadvertent tangents. Turnarounds were quick and the collaboration is sincerely appreciated.

Rather unusually for an author writing about the financial adviser industry, I had a second set of editors review the manuscript. As an investment adviser, portfolio manager, and IIROC registrant, I needed the compliance department at my firm to approve my work. Thanks go out to Kim Shilton, Tracey Stern, Danielle Nichol, and Dan Taylor for their diligence in this regard. I'm especially grateful for Dan's input over the years. He has been given the unenviable task of reviewing countless articles and blog posts written by me and has always provided me with constructive advice, helping me to get my point across in a voice that is uniquely my own. Over the years, several people have told me my tone is too harsh. Dan is one of them. It seems I just can't help it. I really am trying to be respectful in tone while still conveying a sense of more action being needed given the gravity of the problems as I see them. Any lapses in tone are strictly my own fault.

Mark Krause is a friend, client, and brilliant cartoonist. I realized that a book written about unconscious bias might need some "lightening up," so I quickly decided to enlist his help in making the project a little more accessible and a little less serious. The ideas for the captions are his ... all I had to do was tell him what I was looking for in general and he took care of the rest.

There are a number of people who offered input with varying degrees of formality. Abigail Etches offered comments on ESG investing; Jenna Donnelson provided some excellent feedback on the final two chapters, where a political overlay was needed; John "Jazz" Szabo is my best friend and an all-round great guy to bounce ideas off; Lorne Cam, Joe Torszok, and Wayne Wilson are three guys that share common interests, but not always worldviews.

I simply don't know where I would be today were it not for the exceptional vision and leadership of Charlie Spiring. To him and all my

Wellington-Altus colleagues, thank you for letting me onto the team. Every day, I try to live up to your standards.

Brian Smythe is quite possibly the best support associate an adviser could have. Every day, he makes me look good in the eyes of my many excellent clients. Words cannot express how comforting that is.

Thanks to my late dad, who was the best role model a guy like me could have, to my wonderful mom, who is the glue for our family, and to my sweet sister, who shares long walks and her love of family with me as often as she can.

Finally, Olena Brusentsova is the love of my life who saved me when I faced some unexpected challenges. I would not be who I am if not for her enduring love and support. I fell in love with her almost immediately and think she's the absolute best. Then again, I'm biased.

Bibliography

Ackert, Lucy F. "Traditional and Behavioral Finance." In *Foundations of Investor Behavior*, edited by H. Kent Baker and Victor Ricciardi, 25–38. Hoboken, NJ: John Wiley and Sons, 2014.

Ackman, Sharo. "Soldiers with This Trait Are Survivors in Life and War." *Medium*, August 4, 2018. medium.com/@sharonackman/soldiers-with-this -trait-are-survivors-in-war-and-life-2b7c6ad34afb.

Anderson, John, and J. Womack. "Coach Through Biases — Yours and Your Clients'." SEI Investments Company White Paper. Oaks, PA: SEI Investments Company, 2019.

Ariely, Dan. *Predictably Irrational*. New York: Harper Collins, 2008.

Ashworth, Laurence, and Lynnette Purda. *Identifying and Removing Psychological Barriers to Seeking Financial Advice*. Toronto: FP Canada Research Foundation, June 2021.

Barber, Brad M., and Terrence Odean. "Boys Will Be Boys: Gender, Overconfidence and Common Stock Investment." *The Quarterly Journal of Economics* 116, no. 1 (February 2001): 261–92.

Basilico, Elisabetta, and Tommi Johnsen. *Smart(er) Investing: How Academic Insights Propel the Savvy Investor*. Cham, Switzerland: Palgrave Macmillan, 2019.

Beaudry, Paul. *The Great Reset: Supporting the Transition to a Greener, Smarter Economy*. Presentation by the Bank of Canada Deputy Governor, Victoria Forum, August 20, 2020. bankofcanada.ca/wp-content/uploads/2020/08 /presentation-2020-08-20.pdf.

Behavioural Economics in Action at Rotman (BEAR) and Behaviourally Informed Organizations (BI Org). "How to Change: A Conversation: Katy Milkman, in Conversation with Dilip Soman." Transcript of an event on

May 12, 2021. Toronto: Rotman School of Business, 2021. biorgpartnership. com/s/HowToChange-KMilkman-Transcript-1June-310PM.pdf.

Belsky, Gary, and Thomas Gilovich. *Why Smart People Make Big Money Mistakes ... and How to Correct Them: Lessons from the Life-Changing Science of Behavioral Economics.* New York: Fireside, 1999.

Blanchett, David. "The Retirement Mirage." Morningstar Research Paper, 2018.

Burgess, Mark. "Behavioural ETFs Look to Profit from Other Investors' Biases." *Advisor's Edge Magazine*, March 2020.

Carney, Mark. *Value(s): Building a Better World for All.* Toronto: Penguin Random House, 2021.

Crosby, Daniel. *The Behavioral Investor.* New York: Harriman House, 2018.

Dalbar, Inc. *2021 Quantitative Analysis of Investor Behaviour.* Marlborough, MA: Dalbar, 2021.

Dalio, Ray. *Principles for Dealing with the Changing World Order: Why Nations Succeed and Fail.* New York: Simon and Schuster, 2021.

Dubner, Stephen, and Angela Duckworth. "Is 'Toxic Positivity' a Thing?" *No Stupid Questions*, podcast episode 489, January 5, 2022, Freakonomics Radio Network, freakonomics.com/podcast/is-toxic-positivity-a-thing/.

Duke, Annie. *How to Decide: Simple Tools for Making Better Choices.* New York: Portfolio, 2020.

———. *Thinking in Bets: Making Smarter Decisions When You Don't Have All the Facts.* New York: Portfolio, 2019.

Dupras, Martin, et al. *Projection Assumption Guidelines, 2022.* Toronto: FP Canada Standards Council, 2022.

Edesess, Michael. *The Big Investment Lie: What Your Financial Advisor Doesn't Want You to Know.* San Francisco: Berrett Koehler, 2007.

Elkind, Daniel, et al. "When do Investors Freak Out? Machine Learning Predictions of Panic Selling." *Journal of Financial Data Science* 4, no. 1 (Winter 2022): 11–39.

Fama, Eugene F. "Efficient Capital Markets: A Review of Theory and Empirical Work." *Journal of Finance* 25, no. 2 (1970), 383–417.

Fama, Eugene F., and Kenneth R. French, "Multifactor Explanations of Asset Pricing Anomalies." *Journal of Finance* 51, no. 1 (March 1996): 55–84.

Heinberg, Richard. *The End of Growth: Adapting to Our New Economic Reality.* Gabriola Island, B.C.: New Society Publishers, 2011.

Housel, Morgan. *The Psychology of Money: Timeless Lessons on Wealth, Greed, and Happiness.* New York: Harriman House, 2021.

Jackson, Tim. *Prosperity Without Growth: Foundations for the Economy of Tomorrow.* London: Routledge, 2016.

Bibliography

Kahneman, Daniel. *Thinking, Fast and Slow*. Toronto: Doubleday Canada, 2011.

Kahneman, Daniel, and Amos Tversky. "Prospect Theory: An Analysis of Decision Under Risk." *Econometrica* 47, no. 2 (1979): 263–91.

Kahneman, Daniel, Olivier Sibony, and Cass Sunstein. *Noise: A Flaw in Human Judgment*. New York: Little, Brown Spark, 2021.

Kakutani, Michiko. *The Death of Truth: Notes on Falsehood in the Age of Trump*. New York: Tim Duggan Books, 2018.

Kienzler, Mario, Daniel Västfjäll, and Gustav Tinghög. "Individual Differences in Susceptibility to Financial Bullshit." *Journal of Behavioral and Experimental Finance* 34 (June 2022).

Kruger, Justin, and David Dunning. "Unskilled and Unaware of It: How Difficulties in Recognizing One's Own Incompetence Lead to Inflated Self-Assessments." *Journal of Personality and Social Psychology* 77, no. 6 (1999): 1121–34.

Krugman, Paul. *Arguing with Zombies: Economics, Politics, and the Fight for a Better Future*. New York: W.W. Norton, 2020.

Linnainmaa, Juhani T., Brian T. Melzer, and Alessandro Previtero. "The Misguided Beliefs of Financial Advisors." *Journal of Finance* 76, no. 2 (April 2021): 587–621.

MacDonald, Bonnie-Jeanne, Marvin Avery, and Richard J. Morrison. *The "Risk" of Ignoring Risks in Retirement Financial Planning*. Toronto: FP Canada Standards Council, March 2018.

Marks, Howard. *Mastering the Market Cycle: Getting the Odds on Your Side*. New York: Harper Business, 2018.

Montmarquette, Claude, and Nathalie Viennot-Briot. "The Gamma Factors and the Value of Financial Advice." *Annals of Economics and Finance* 20, no. 1 (2019): 387–411.

Nordell, Jessica. *The End of Bias: A Beginning: The Science and Practice of Overcoming Unconscious Bias*. New York: Metropolitan Books, 2021.

Odean, Terrance. "Are Investors Reluctant to Realize Their Losses?" *Journal of Finance* 53, no. 5: 1775–98.

Pennycock, Gordon, et al. "On the Reception and Detection of Pseudo-Profound Bullshit." *Judgement and Decision Making* 10, no. 6 (November 2015): 549–63.

Sah, Sunita, Prashant Malaviya, and Debora Thompson. "Conflict of Interest Disclosure as an Expertise Cue: Differential Effects due to Automatic Versus Deliberative Processing." *Organizational Behavior and Human Decision Processes* 147 (2018): 127–46.

Sharpe, William F. "The Arithmetic of Active Management." *Financial Analysts Journal* 47, no. 1 (Jan/Feb 1991): 7–9.

Shiller, Robert. *Irrational Exuberance: Revised and Expanded Third Edition.* Princeton: Princeton University Press, 2016.

———. *Narrative Economics: How Stories Go Viral and Drive Major Economic Events.* Princeton: Princeton University Press, 2020.

Somers, Moira. *Advice That Sticks: How to Give Financial Advice that People Will Follow.* London: Practical Inspiration Publishing, 2018.

Spratt, David, and Alia Armistead. *Fatal Calculations: How Economics Has Underestimated Climate Damage and Encouraged Inaction.* Melbourne, Australia: National Centre for Climate Restoration, April 2020.

Stern, Nicholas. *The Economics of Climate Change: The Stern Review.* Cambridge: Cambridge University Press, 2006.

Stewart, Rosemary. *Choices for the Manager: A Guide to Managerial Work and Behaviour.* Toronto: McGraw-Hill, 1982.

Taleb, Nassim Nicholas. *Fooled by Randomness: The Hidden Role of Chance in Life and in the Markets.* New York: Texere, 2001.

Thaler, Richard. *Misbehaving: The Story of Behavioral Economics.* New York: Norton, 2015.

Thaler, Richard, and Cass Sunstein. *Nudge: The Final Edition.* New York: Penguin, 2021.

Thompson, John R.J., et al. "Know Your Clients' Behaviours: A Cluster Analysis of Financial Transactions." *Journal of Risk and Financial Management* 14, no. 2: 50. mdpi.com/1911-8074/14/2/50/htm.

Victor, Peter. *Managing Without Growth: Slower by Design, not Disaster.* Toronto: Edward Elgar, 2008.

Index

Index

About the Author

John De Goey, CFP, CIM, FP Canada Fellow, is an acclaimed portfolio manager with Wellington-Altus Private Wealth in Toronto. He has written for several national publications including the *Globe and Mail* and the *National Post* and has made several appearances on a variety of television networks including CBC's *The National* and CTV's *Canada AM*. Much like *Bullshift*, his previous books, *The Professional Financial Advisor* and *STANDUP to the Financial Services Industry*, explored the topics of professionalism, transparency, and unconscious bias, with an emphasis on improving client-adviser interaction.

John is both a thought leader and a passionate advocate for investor education and purposeful working relationships. He believes decisions should be made using the best available evidence, which leads to lifelong learning and a better understanding of capital markets. Visit John's advisory website at standupadvisors.ca and his personal website, which includes writing and podcasts, at standup.today.